Let
Harry
Become
Sally

KELLY R. NOVAK

Let

Harry

Become

Sally

Responding to the

Anti-Transgender Moment

Let Harry Become Sally

Hypothesis Press
Andover, MA
www.HypothesisPress.com

ISBN-13: 978-1948785051
ISBN-10: 1948785056

For Harrys and Sallys everywhere

Contents

Preface

In part due to the right's backlash that came with the increased Civil Rights for LGBT citizens during the Obama administration, followed by the election of Trump, which emboldened hate groups of all kinds, anti-transgender thoughts, actions, laws, articles, and books have been on the rise. IMHO, a good example is Ryan T. Anderson's *When Harry Became Sally*.

Had I opted to write a book on transgender Civil Rights and the misinformation being shared by transphobic authors and organizations, to share actual research, to counter the myths being used against the transgender population, to write a book sympathetic to them, I would have done so in a very different format than this parody. Here, I am keeping the same format and chapter structures. I am also using "transgender" here to mean someone with a gender identity different enough from their assigned sex to cause gender dysphoria, and LGBT is inclusive (LGBTQIA+).

What is most troublesome about books like *When Harry Became Sally* is that many people are actually taking the biased opinions in the books seriously.

And that is worrisome—being used as an "authoritative" book on the subject. It posits that transgendered people should unilaterally be denied medical care. It argues that transgendered people be explicitly excluded from Civil Rights legislation.

We will see that, as written in a New York Times Op Ed,[1] that the book "suggests that transgender people are crazy, and that what we [transgendered people] deserve at every turn is scorn, contempt and belittlement."

1

The book is even detrimental to transgender children by the insistence that they be denied medically necessary treatment, and instead be forced into the "wrong" puberty—one that will give them increased depression rather that happiness.

The book appears to be heavily based on ideology rather than science, and makes heavy use of the opinions of a small group of anti-transgender activists.

Yet, on page 46, Anderson writes (in all seriousness):

> What does it even mean to have an internal sense of gender? What does gender feel like? What meaning can we give to the concept of sex and gender, apart from having the body of a particular sex?

He wrote *When Harry Became Sally* as if he were an expert on gender identity, yet, he boasts that *he does not even know what gender identity is!*

I am giving Dr. Anderson no disrespect in his abilities as a journalist, author, chief propagandist, father of the year, or whatever he identifies himself as. We should respect one another's identities. However, in his defense of his book against the critique in the aforesaid Op Ed, he writes:[2]

> Boylan claims I wrote "a book that suggests that transgender people are crazy, and that what we [people who identify as transgender] deserve at every turn is *scorn, contempt, and belittlement.*"
> **Good luck finding a single line from my book to back up either claim**. I wrote nothing of the sort...
> Ford immediately jumped to Boylan's defense on Twitter, writing: "You call them mentally ill." I replied: "Simple. **Please quote the passage where I 'call them mentally ill.'** You can't quote that passage because it doesn't exist." (emphasis added)

And finally, also in his defense, he writes:

> Boylan claims my book is "abundant in junk science," but couldn't point to anything in particular that I got wrong.

I respectfully accept the challenge.

Introduction

Transgender people have existed for millennia. Often, they were accepted as who they were, rather than persecuted. We see many examples of this.

In 2011, a grave was unearthed in the Czech Republic where an anatomic male was buried as a female.[1] We read:

> The male skeleton was found in a suburb of Prague and is buried in a manner previously only seen for female burials. The body is believed to date from between 2900 and 2500BC and is from the Corded Ware culture of the Copper Age...
>
> Kamila Remišová, the head of the research team, said: "From history and ethnology, we know that when a culture had strict burial rules they never made mistakes with these sort of things."
>
> Archaeologist Kateřina Semrádová told *Czech Position*: "We believe this is one of the earliest cases of what could be described as a 'transsexual' or 'third gender grave' in the Czech Republic."
>
> This is not the first time a skeleton has been found buried as a member of the opposite sex. One woman from the Mesolithic period, who was assumed to be a warrior, was found buried with weapons.

The article also mentions that a Mesolithic burial was unearthed with a possible female-to-male body.

Hijra, transgendered people in what is now known as India, Bangladesh, and Pakistan, have existed for thousands of years.[2] Sometimes known as a third sex, first mentioned—and they are celebrated—in ancient Hindu texts such as the *Mahabharata* and the *Kama Sutra*.[3] And transgender people are not rare in India. In 2014, India's census counted nearly one half of one million, including 55,000 children.[4]

In pre-Columbian America, two-spirit people were common. They did not live according to traditional gender roles, and were often considered blessed and revered.[5]

Transgender people existed in ancient Roman times.[6] The 3rd Century Roman Emperor Elagabalus was transgender and used female titles.[7] She is recorded as willing to offer half of the empire to any surgeon who could correct her genitalia to female.[8]

In the 18th Century, the French aristocrat and soldier Chevalier d'Eon de Beaumont legally transitions and changes her name to Charlotte-Genevieve-Louise-Auguste-Andree-Timothee d'Eon de Beaumont.[9]

Natal females lived as men in countless cultures and ages. Some transgender men fought in American wars. Over 200 natal females fought in the US Civil War, some of whom were transgender and lived as men,[10] including Albert Cashier, pictured.[11]

In the early 1930s, Lili Elbe had an early form of sex reassignment surgery.[12] She became a sensation, but she was not the first: Dr Alan L. Hart had female-to-male surgery in 1917,[13] and Dora R had female-to-male surgery shortly before Elbe.[14]

Christine Jorgensen had gender affirming surgery in the early 1950s. She was quite a celebrity after that.

In 1956, Dr. Georges Burou opened his gender affirming surgery clinic in Casablanca.[15] Over 3,000 patients had their affirming surgery there.

Newer techniques have been developed and many thousands of people with Gender Dysphoria have been helped by transition and surgery since.

Gender Dysphoria is a serious condition where a person's gender identity conflicts with their sex assigned at birth. It can lead to suicide if not treated. Fortunately, treatment is often available for those that can afford it. In many countries, especially European, treatment is available for all due to Universal Health Care. A step towards Universal Health Care was made in the USA during the Obama administration, but the Trump administration is turning that back.

Also, since Trump's election, hate groups have felt emboldened and hate crimes are on the rise.[16] Among this backlash against minority rights is a growing anti-LGBT sentiment.

A best-selling book, named *When Harry Became Sally* by Ryan T. Anderson, argues against the medical treatment of transgender patients. It is now being used extensively in the Conservative blogosphere to justify the refusal of health care to transgender patients and even to delegitimize their identities.

Roger Severino, who coauthored a paper with Ryan T. Anderson in 2016 arguing that health care workers should be allowed to refuse to treat transgender patients,[17] is now the director of the Department of Health and Human Services' Office for Civil Rights (the OCR). We might now call it the "Office of Civil Wrongs." In 2016, before he took office, the OCR clarified that the law bars discrimination against transgender people, or any bias based on gender identity, in section 1557.[18] A federal judge blocked this, meaning that health care discrimination against transgender people is not illegal. Severino has been greatly strengthening and expanding protections for health care providers who have objections to treating certain people or performing procedures.[19]

When asked whether the conscience-protection efforts would shield those who refuse to provide hormone therapy or other treatments for transgender patients, Serevino replied, "to the fullest extent."[20]

In February 2018, Ryan T. Anderson published the book, *When Harry Became Sally*, relying heavily on biased opinons, including that of Paul McHugh, and misrepresented a 2011 Swedish study on transgender outcomes. In step, Eric Teetsel, president of the anti-LGBT Family Policy Alliance of Kansas, penned one of the most heinous declarations of hate against transgender people, a resolution to "oppose all efforts to validate transgender identity." He cited the biased McHugh work and the misrepresented Swedish study mentioned in the *When Harry Became Sally: Responding to the Transgender Moment* book as reasons for doing so.[21]

The following month, President Trump reiterated his declaration that transgender people cannot serve in the military.

Also in step with Anderson's *Responding to the Transgender Moment* book is the anti-transgender manifesto *Understanding and Responding to the Transgender Movement*[22] by the hate group[23] Family Research Council (FRC), outlying a five point plan of attack against the transgender population. Huffpost described FRC's manifesto in their article, *And Then They Came for Transgender People*[24] as:

> When the anti-transgender student bill in South Dakota passed, it was the first step in a plan to eradicate transgender people from American life. Last year, the Family Research Council laid out a five point plan to legislate transgender people out of existence by making the

legal, medical, and social climate too hostile for anyone to transition in.

1. States and the federal government should not allow legal gender marker changes.

2. Transgender people should not have any legal protections against discrimination, nor should anyone be forced to respect their identity.

3. Transgender people should not be legally allowed to use facilities in accordance with their gender identity.

4. Medical coverage related to transition should not be provided by the government, or any other entity.

5. Transgender people should not be allowed to serve in the military.

Stop for a moment here, and imagine a world where you can't get an accurate government ID. A world where you can't vote, can't drive without risking arrest, and can't get a job. You cannot prove that you are who you are, because no one will believe your ID is real. You will never be treated as your correct gender by any government agency. What ID you have will constantly out you as transgender, inviting discrimination. Perfectly legal discrimination, if part two of their plan succeeds.

Now imagine being constantly outed as transgender in this world where the law explicitly states that you are a target. Imagine having that scarlet A on every ID you possess making it clear that the bearer of this card is sub-human and has no rights: fire them, kick them out of their home, refuse to serve them, take their children away, verbally abuse them for your amusement at work—it's all good. The religious "liberty" to abuse, harass, and humiliate transgender people reigns supreme in the Family Research Council's brave new transgender-free world.

Now imagine being transgender, and that on top of being legally un-personed, jobless, homeless, harassed, and hated, you'll be arrested for using a bathroom. Use one bathroom, and it's a felony. Use the other, and you're likely to be beaten, maybe to death. If you fight back against your attackers, you'll go to a prison for people of the opposite gender, that guarantees you will continue to be raped, beaten, and denied medical care.

Imagine that on top of all of this, you can't get treatment for gender dysphoria other than (medically debunked, ineffective, counter-productive) religious-based reparative therapy. Unable to medically transition, the only proven treatment for gender dysphoria, you're marked constantly as being transgender. Not only does your ID mark you as an undesirable, everything on the outside of your body does too.

To add insult to injury, you can't even join the Army to escape the inevitable poverty and homelessness that accompanies being transgender under their plan.

Given all of these factors, the goal of the FRC couldn't be clearer: transgender people must be eradicated from American life. Either stay in the closet, or be un-personed in a legal sense. Trans people who transition will marginalized in education, and shoved towards the underground economy. Transgender people will be forced to disappear to where all the other ragged people go: into storm drains, under bridges, and to encampments on the fringes of society. The Family Research Council and Republicans know full well that most transgender people, when faced with the certainty of personal ruin, will remain alone, in the closet, for life.

However short that may be.

America is in the midst of an "Anti-Transgender Moment." Within two years, the "right" of conservative and religious Americans to dismiss the identities of, discriminate against, and refuse treatment for, transgender people has become a cause claiming the mantle of civil rights.

A meme for this backlash is "biology isn't bigotry," and that those born transgender should just accept their assigned sex and live in the gender role of such sex. But would they object to a baby born with a heart defect getting heart surgery? Would they object to someone who was born deaf getting a cochlear implant? "No, God made you deaf; getting a cochlear implant will send you straight to hell." Or not? If God made someone diabetic, should they be refused insulin?

Most physicians who treat transgender patients will help them transition if (and hopefully only if) it will help them. There are rare dissenters. Paul McHugh is one of them. As mentioned in *When Harry Became Sally*, Dr. McHugh argued [falsely] that transition and surgery does not help transgender patients.

In this book, I argue that McHugh got it wrong. Palliative treatments such as transition, hormone therapy, and up to and including gender affirming surgeries are often more beneficial treatment for appropriate transgender candidates. Denial of such treatments can lead to depression, substance abuse, and even suicide. It is morally repugnant to deny medical care to a class of patients.

In the first chapter, I will focus on the anti-transgender moment in law, medicine, and morality. It looks at what was once common sense and how recent developments might look, on the surface, to be sensible, but are actually harmful not just to transgender people, but innocent cisgender bystanders.

In the second chapter, I will let anti-transgender activists speak for themselves. It can be quite revealing.

After listening to anti-transgender activists, we will hear from their victims—those who were refused treatment or affirmation. We will also hear from those who were allowed to transition and we will see that transition is often a good, not a bad, treatment.

11

Chapter four lays out the foundation on how medical treatment for transgender patients is most frequently highly beneficial. Contrary to the activists, gender identity isn't simply "assigned" at birth. It is inborn. It may be binary and unchangeable, or it might be in-between male-identified and female-identified.

Chapter five looks at the treatments themselves and the benefits of such treatments. Denial of care can be dangerous to the individual.

Chapter six focuses on early treatment. How often do gender-nonconforming children "grow out of it," and what are the benefits of early transitioning? What are the harms of treatment denial?

Chapter seven takes a brief look at gender. What does it mean? What has gender meant through the years? It asks what Ryan T. Anderson's point was with the chapter (I don't get it).

Chapter eight discusses public policy. How should the anti-transgender moment be addressed? What laws would be suitable for all?

Anti-transgender ideology may be establishing a firm place in American culture, and they act as if their "truths" are self-evident. But they are not. Even if this anti-transgender moment is fleeting (we should hope so), that does not mean that we should idly stand by and watch as our transgender family members, friends, and colleagues are trampled upon. We need to insist on telling the truth to prevent people's lives from being irreparably harmed.

CHAPTER ONE

Our Anti-Transgender Moment

Before North Carolina's "bathroom bill", few had thoughts about people using the "wrong" restroom. Women used the women's room and men used the men's room. How was it decided who enters which room? By legality. Legal women used the women's room. Likewise for men. It was frequently illegal (except for maintenance or emergencies or helping those in need) for a man to use a women's restroom and vice versa.

When in doubt, such as the case of a "butch" woman or a feminine male, a gatekeeper such as a manager or police officer could ask for identification. Does the "M" or "F" on the ID match the sign on the door? If so, no foul, except for the embarrassment of the victim who was asked for the ID by the busybody twit who couldn't keep their nose out of it. But these cases were rare.

Now, however, with "bathroom bills" popping up in any US states, the legality of transgender people using appropriate restrooms is in question and often illegal. And the victims are not just transgender people. Cisgender people are getting caught and victimized as well.

The "bathroom bills" not only deny transgender citizens from using the appropriate restroom, but allow them to use the opposite gender restroom. Does that make sense? Rather than allowing people to use appropriate restrooms, the laws put men in women's rooms and women in men's rooms. Those who have had surgery would be required to use opposite gender restrooms or none at all. For instance, Virginia's bill[1] requires people to use the facility according to their sex where *"Sex" means the physical condition of being male or female as shown on an individual's original birth certificate.*

A popular meme[2] that displays this perversion of justice is:

Kelly Lauren
Houston, do you REALLY want me in the same restroom as your husband or boyfriend?
— with Alyson Calagna and Tayda Lebon.

Does that look right? The man in the photo on the right is Michael C. Hughes. He writes, "Do I look like I belong in women's facilities? Republicans are trying to get legislation passed that would put me there, based on my gender at birth. Trans people aren't going to the bathroom to spy on you, or otherwise cause you harm, #wejustneedtopee."[3]

There is collateral damage to cisgender people as well. What happens when a not-so-feminine woman uses the women's facilities? These innocent women have been harassed, thrown out of facilities, and even arrested due to this new fear that transgender people might try to use public facilities.

A cis woman, Cortney Bogorad was kicked out of Detroit's Fishbones restaurant after she attempted to use the women's bathroom. A security guard pushed her up against the wall and accused her of being a "boy."[4] She stated, "As I came out of the stall, this gentleman—who was a security guard—came in the bathroom, and before I was even completely out of the bathroom he grabbed me by the arms and pushed me up against the wall, told me that boys aren't allowed in this restroom. . . ."

In her Facebook post on Aug. 8, Julie Bidwell was out with her girlfriend, Heather Hess, enjoying a few drinks at Kildare's Irish Pub in Scranton when things took a terrible turn. She posted:[5]

"I was kicked out of my first bar tonight.. Well, allowed back in after i argued with the bouncer who kicked me out.. I went to the bathroom with a friend, then came out to a bouncer saying i had to leave bc men arent allowed in the girls bathroom.. I had to plead with him for almost a minute that i was a girl.. I was sober when it happened, n i am embarrassed enough to never go back.. The manager was even a bigger jerk than the bouncer... Kildare's in Scranton, i will never come back, thank you."

In April 2016, a man illegally barged into a women's restroom at Baylor Medical Center to make sure that Jessica Rush, a cisgendered woman who manages a local health-food takeout place, was peeing in the proper place.[6] Jessica wears her hair short and the man harassed her because he thought that she might be a boy. Note that it was the anti-trans advocate that violated the law and that an innocent ciswomen was the victim.

In May 2016, a cisgendered woman was beaten for looking too masculine, as bystanders stood by and watched.[7] We read:

Brittany Nicole Wallace wrote, "Today I was assaulted. A man assaulted me because I look like a 'dike'! He told me that he would 'beat me like the man I want to be.' He said, 'people like me make him hate the world.'"
"He started by hitting me over and over in the face until he got me down," Wallace wrote. "After I was down he began to kick me in the stomach, side, and face."

Wallace said she tried to fight back, but her attacker was bigger and stronger. Bystanders, she said, never even lifted a finger to help.

"The sad part is that no one would come help me either. Several people stood around and watched this happen to me. Again, I truly believe that if I had a more feminine appearance someone would have helped," she wrote.

The article concluded:

Anti-LGBT violence is on the rise in the U.S. as conservatives ratchet up the fear-mongering and violent rhetoric around transgender equality, public restrooms and non-existent threats to children by trans men and women.

Also in May 2016, Aimee Toms, who has a pixie haircut because she had, for the third time, donated her hair to a charity that makes wigs for child cancer patients, was harassed in a women's room in a Walmart.[8] The article states:

Aimee Toms was washing her hands in the women's bathroom at Walmart in Danbury Friday when a stranger approached her and said, "You're disgusting!" and "You don't belong here!"

After momentary confusion, she realized that the woman next to her thought - because of her pixie-style haircut and baseball cap - that she was transgender.

Toms believes the incident happened because of the national controversy sparked by a law that was passed in North Carolina attempting to force transgender people to use the bathroom of the gender they were identified as at birth.

In Miami, a cis woman (a mother of three children) was arrested. When assigning her a place of incarceration, they opted to examine her vagina in case she may be transgender. She was not, but the appearance of her vagina had "non-traditional male characteristics" (perhaps making them think that she was post-op male-to-female) and jailed her in a common cell with 40 men who reportedly sexually harassed her.[9]

The list goes on regarding cisgender people harassed and jailed for not being feminine or masculine enough, and thus are assumed to be (and punished for "being") transgender.

While the laws may be meant to harm only the transgender population, cisgender citizens are being harmed in the way. Is this collateral damage fine with the anti-trans activists?

North Carolina's HB2, and other "Bathroom Bills", are as Chris Wallace said, "a solution in search of a problem."[10] The Fox News host then noted that Politifact was unable to find any instances of people using laws meant to protect transgender people as cover for committing a crime.

The Battle against Transgender Troops

In 2015, the Department of Defense asked the RAND Corporation to initiate a study on the implications of allowing transgender personnel to serve openly.[11] The study concluded that if the U.S. military decides to let transgender people serve openly, the number would likely be a small fraction of the total force and have minimal impact on readiness and health care costs.[12]

The US government then removed the ban on transgender military members, and some trans soldiers began serving openly.

Then in 2017, the new president, in a tweet,[13] declared that:

After consultation with my Generals and military experts, please be advised that the United States Government will

17

not accept or allow Transgender individuals to serve in any capacity in the U.S. Military.

Who were these "experts" upon whom the president is relying? Mainly, it is VP Pence and fellow anti-trans activists. We read:[14]

> Yet behind the scenes, a "panel of experts" has been crafting a report, also released on Friday, designed to provide pretextual justification for Trump's ban. According to multiple sources, Vice President Mike Pence played a leading role in the creation of this report, along with **Ryan Anderson, an anti-trans activist**, and Tony Perkins, head of the Family Research Council, an anti-LGBTQ lobbying group. (emphasis added)

The Family Research Council is a hate group.[15]

The report[16] suggested a ban for allowing transgender people to transition as well as to ban medical treatment for it. It misconstrued the 2015 Dhejne study and this misrepresentation is included in Anderson's book. It concluded that *Transgender Persons Who Require or Have Undergone Gender Transition Are Disqualified*; and *Transgender Persons With a History or Diagnosis of Gender Dysphoria Are Disqualified, Except Under Certain Limited Circumstances*.

This is ideology, not science. And it did cause controversy. In *The Hill*,[17] we read:

> "Although you state that the panel received input from civilian medical professionals, the recommendations appear to us to be inconsistent with what we have heard from the civilian medical community," the lawmakers write.
>
> "Numerous recognized experts, former military officials and Surgeons General, and organizations representing medical professionals have released statements criticizing

the Report's recommendations and the underlying scientific basis for these recommendations."

The report's analysis of medical research has been harshly criticized as misrepresenting the findings or leaving out important context. The American Medical Association, the country's largest medical organization, told Mattis in a letter that his recommendations "mischaracterized and rejected" evidence on treatment for gender dysphoria.

The fact that anti-trans activists have been able to influence White House policy to the point of deliberately harming transgender citizens should be cause for alarm. Bigotry has no place in national policy.

CHAPTER TWO

What the Activists Babble

A nti-transgender activists' statements are generally based on ideology, rather than science. We will get to the science in subsequent chapters. For now, let us examine their echo chamber.

One tool that anti-transgender activists use against their victims is the idea that they are evil. In reality, transgender people just want to get on with their lives.

In the ThinkProgress article *How The Incendiary Rhetoric Against Transgender Youth Is Escalating*,[1] we read:

> Conservatives are continuing to ramp up their rhetoric against transgender youth, using the Pacific Justice Institute's (PJI) fabricated story about Colorado teen Jane Doe to justify overturning California's new law protecting transgender students. All Jane seemed to do is go the bathroom, but her mere existence and use of the school facilities seems to be agitating conservatives to use some particularly incendiary rhetoric.
>
> Disgraced[2] Navy Chaplain Gordon Klingenschmitt, who recently announced he's running for state office in Colorado, added to the attacks on Jane this week, accusing her of "raping — at least visually — these teenage girls"
>
> KLINGENSCHMITT: Now the public school children are being told by a demonic spirit, "You must open up your daughter's privacy to our perversion." And this demonic spirit inside of this boy is now violating, and for all intents and purposes, he's raping — at least visually — these teenage girls.

It continues:

> David Kupelian, managing editor of the uber-conservative
> site WorldNetDaily, offered his own concern this week
> about Coy Mathis, the six-year-old Colorado trans student
> who also successfully fought for the right to use the
> bathroom...
> KUPELIAN: This is a transgender six-year-old. Look,
> this is child abuse: to go and tell this six-year-old child who
> was born a boy is actually a girl, but they sued and they won.
> This is sort of the new emerging civil rights movement, as
> ghoulish as it seems — it's just in time for Halloween I guess.

Scott Lively, former state director for the California branch
of American Family Association, which Southern Poverty
Law Center named a Hate Group[3], states[4]:

> "Ultimately, the 'gay' agenda is simply a sub-plot of the
> larger Satanic agenda and now that LGBTQ goals appear
> nearly fully realized, the hidden hands behind them (both
> human and demonic) are coming into view. The puppet-
> masters who have made 'gay' supremacy possible have been
> working backward from the branch to the root to bring
> chaos out of order — the ultimate satanic goal: first
> confusion of sexuality as conduct, then confusion of
> marriage and family, then confusion of gender, and next
> confusion of what the Bible calls 'kinds.' It is not just the
> deconstruction of civilization but the dissolution of all
> boundaries between human and animal and machine, to
> produce creatures that are a blend of all three. We are
> witnessing the end-game before our very eyes but few
> recognize what they are seeing. What is next in the LGBTQ
> agenda is transhumanism, the redefinition of humanness
> and emergence of human/animal/machine chimeral forms.
> Satan is fashioning a final comprehensive counterfeit
> alternative to the creation over which Man finally assumes
> that he has accessed the Tree of Life and is persuaded that
> he is God, destroying himself and 'goodness' itself in the
> process."

Activists also like to claim that transgender people are insane. Fox News contributor Keith Ablow Said he considers Chaz Bono's transition "a psychotic delusion--a fixed and false belief," adding that there is "nothing substantially different from a woman believing she is a man than there is about a woman believing she is a CIA agent being followed by the KGB (when in reality, she is, say, a salesperson at J. Crew)."[5]

Further, he compared being trans to a person pretending he or she is a farm animal: "Here's an analogy: If a person came to me tattooed as a zebra - Zebraman... go on TV, but if you want me to agree with you that you're a zebra, well now you're invading my reality... It's dancing with a woman as a man."[6]

Anti-transgender activist Dr. Paul McHugh said that transgenderism is a "mental disorder" that merits treatment, and that people who promote sexual reassignment surgery are collaborating with and promoting a mental disorder.[7]

Others simply state that being transphobic is totally normal and cool. In *Transphobia Is Perfectly Natural*, Gavin McInnes writes:[8]

> When Janet Mock appears on MSNBC and talks about growing up as a black chick, nobody's going to bat an eye. We'll all be totally comfortable with him retroactively rewriting history and putting a skirt on all his boyhood memories.
>
> I kid. I kid. Of course it's fucking unusual. We're all transphobic. We aren't blind. We see there are no old trannies. They die of drug overdoses and suicide way before they're 40 and nobody notices because nobody knows them. They are mentally ill gays who need help, and that help doesn't include being maimed by physicians. These aren't women trapped in a man's body. They are nuts trapped in a crazy person's body...

23

By pretending this is all perfectly sane, you are enabling these poor bastards to mutilate themselves. This insane war on pronouns is about telling people what to do... To justify trannies is to allow mentally ill people to mutilate themselves. When your actions are getting people mutilated, you're at war with them.

The Echo Chamber

Anti-transgender activists utilized by Ryan T. Anderson often rely on "studies" by (mainly opinions of) a small group of very biased people and organizations. They may be talented scholars and scientists, and by no means to I wish to demean their integrity or scholarship and especially not their reputation, and am not denouncing them. But their own actions show bias against transgendered people, and thus I will treat them as suspect when it comes to posting what is actually best for the trans community. I will refer to them as "the gang."

These include:

1. The so-called American College of Pediatricians (ACPeds). Despite the name, they are described by the Southern Poverty Law Center as an extremist anti-LGBT hate group.[9] They state "ACPeds opposes adoption by LGBT couples, links homosexuality to pedophilia, endorses so-called reparative or sexual orientation conversion therapy for homosexual youth, believes transgender people have a mental illness and has called transgender health care for youth child abuse." They should not be confused with the much larger, and legitimate, American Academy of Pediatrics.

2. Dr. Lawrence Mayer. He was paid $400/hour as an expert witness for North Carolina in its "transgender bathroom" lawsuit.[10] He argued FOR the anti-

transgender legislation. This shows anti-trans bias. Worse, he coauthored the infamous *New Atlantis* pseudoscience "Study".[11]

3. Dr. Paul McHugh. Infamously known for shutting down the clinic at Johns Hopkins, he is a rare anti-transgender psychiatrist, and is thus heavily quoted by activists. Anti-trans sins of his include coauthoring a misleading declaration *Gender Ideology Harms Children*[12] for the aforesaid hate group ACPeds, and coauthoring with Mayer the *New Atlantis* propaganda piece.

   Another infamous work of his is the confusing yet highly insulting 2004 *Surgical Sex* opinion piece in *First Things*.[13] In response to it, Jennifer Usher writes:[14]

   > One wonders why Dr. McHugh would choose such a cruel approach to the treatment of transsexuals. Sex-reassignment surgery has proven to be the only successful treatment for these patients, and yet for some reason he wishes to deny this. He makes a rather clumsy attempt to justify his position by comparing the treatment of adults who are transsexual with the treatment of children who are intersexed. Ironically, the arguments for one contradict the arguments for the other. Children who are intersexed have traditionally been surgically altered in whatever manner is simplest. This has often resulted in a child who has a male brain being given a female body. As Dr. McHugh points out, such a child is tormented by the attempt to force him to live at odds with his natural inclinations. And yet, he cannot find the compassion to provide treatment to those who, for whatever reason, were born male but whose brains were not sexualized as male in the womb. Even though both groups face the same set of problems, Dr. McHugh sets out to protect one group while effectively punishing the other.

4. Walt Heyer. Walt was not transgender, yet had surgery and transitioned anyway. That is unfortunate, and it does show that some people who do manage to obtain surgery are not appropriate candidates. On page 70 of *When Harry Became Sally,* Walt describes that he later learned that he had, instead, dissociative disorder.

In turn, he became a darling of the anti-trans movement. Since transitioning was not good for him, the anti-trans activists claim that it is good for no one, and seek to prevent others from transitioning. This is akin to one person having a penicillin allergy and declaring that no one should be able to be treated with penicillin. Or, a lactose-intolerant person seeking to ban milk.

Walt has become a serious anti-trans activist, and writes anti-trans screed after screed on anti-LGBT sites including Public Discourse[15] and The Daily Signal.[16]

In *"Billy" - Recycling anti-gay to anti-trans*, we read:[17]

> Heyer's dozen posts all say the same thing: Transgender — bad. He never offers any proof of anything and he never cites peer-reviewed research. Heyer sometimes speaks of people who have supposedly contacted him regretting their transition. We have no way of knowing — and Anderson has no way of knowing — if these people even exist...
>
> There is usually one reason that people become transgender which is to mitigate the effects of gender dysphoria. Heyer is asserting that there is an underlying psychological cause for gender dysphoria; one that the psychiatric profession is ignoring or even obscuring. Now if we could only know and treat that underlying cause...
>
> Sound familiar? It is the conspiracy theory of James Dobson and others 20 years ago. Their crackpot theories provided (and continue to provide) the foundation for conversion therapy.

26

Heyer and Ryan T. Anderson are trying to do the same thing in regards to gender identity. Conversion therapy exists to support religious oriented discrimination. A rationale (the underlying cause of sexuality that they do not approve of) came after the fact.

5. Paul Hruz. Hruz is an "expert" witness[18] for the hate group,[19] Alliance Defending Freedom. He testifies AGAINST trans people and their cases. But his testimony is only anti-trans opinion. We read,[20]

> *Dr. Hruz is an Associate Professor of Pediatrics in the Division of Pediatric Endocrinology and Diabetes at Washington University School of Medicine in St. Louis. He is proffered as an expert witness based on his study of "existing literature related to the incidence, potential etiology and treatment of gender dysphoria."* ... Translated, it appears to mean that he has read some things about it. Dr. Hruz admits that he has not treated any transgender patients, patients with gender dysphoria, conducted peer-reviewed research about gender identity, transgender people, or gender dysphoria; and is not a psychiatrist, a psychologist, nor mental health care provider of any kind, who could speak knowledgeably about the effects of Defendant's discriminatory policy on transgender students, let alone Plaintiff.

6. Michelle Cretella. Cretella is the president of the hate group ACPeds mentioned above.[21] She also writes scathing attacks against transgender people.[22] The Society for Adolescent Health and Medicine wrote a lengthy rebuttal against one of her attacks. In *SAHM Responds to Dr. Michelle Cretella*, we read:[23]

> The Society for Adolescent Health and Medicine strongly rejects the views of those in the medical

community pushing political and ideological agendas not based on science and facts.

Recently, Dr. Michelle Cretella, the president of the American College of Pediatricians, penned a scathing attack on the transgender community thinly veiled as an argument against the dangers of transgender surgery and support; an argument based on medical omissions, circumstantial facts, hateful interpretation and peripheral context.

Earlier this month, the Adolescent Health News Roundup, compiled by Multiview and distributed by SAHM, included the article "I'm a Pediatrician. How Transgender Ideology Has Infiltrated My Field and Produced Large-Scale Child Abuse". While SAHM welcomes opposing views and tries to include other perspectives in its weekly digest of news culled from around the internet, SAHM does not condone misinformation and hurtful, ideological opinion, not rooted in science or evidence-based medicine. The above-referenced article does not meet these standards and was included as "news" in error. It not only promotes a biased agenda, but does so with outright disregard for the facts. We sincerely apologize for including this alongside legitimate news stories and are currently revising our procedures to ensure this does not happen again.

Dr. Cretella begins with "What doctors once treated as a mental illness, the medical community now largely affirms and even promotes as normal." She fails to reference historical medical errors with regard to mental illness such as hysteria, a catch-all diagnosis for outspoken women; nostalgia, an affliction to those who had left their home; or the color purple, once argued to drive people insane. She then lists eight "basic facts" which are anything but, and ends with a conclusion of "Transition-affirming protocol is child abuse."

They then debunk every one of her points one by one.

28

Again, the "gang" may be well-educated and talented, but their work goes against most other professionals' opinions. They may (or may not) have honest motives for what they do. But when we read trans articles, books, and "studies" that rarely venture out of the gang's echo chamber, one should be suspicious not only of their conclusions but also of their motives.

The New Atlantis "Study"

In the Fall of 2016, Mayer and McHugh co-authored and the report *Sexuality and Gender Findings from the Biological, Psychological, and Social Sciences* in *The New Atlantis*, a non-peer-reviewed journal. In it, the authors bring up and discuss quite a number of interesting studies. Many are rather interesting. However, their conclusions do not at all seem based on all of the mentioned studies. They appear to be their own opinions, and they are anti-trans.

Such a "study" is both pseudoscience and propaganda. A lay person might skim it and believe the authors' conclusions. The lengthy screed appears to be an attempt to "baffle 'em with bullshit."

McHugh even admitted that it was an opinion piece for lay people:[24]

> In a wide-ranging phone interview, the Johns Hopkins professor disputed the importance of peer review for the *New Atlantis* report—"It's an opinion piece for the general public."

ThinkProgress addressed the anti-trans "study" in *The Truth About The Massive New Study That Has Captivated Anti-LGBT Groups: A new report that seems*

to contradict the basics of LGBT identity falls totally flat.
In the lengthy article, they state:[25]

> Anti-LGBT conservative outlets have been abuzz this week about a new report that seems suspiciously designed to make it look like those who oppose LGBT equality have science on their side.
>
> They don't.
>
> The "Sexuality and Gender" special report, published by The *New Atlantis*, claims to undermine the belief that LGBT people are "born that way." It purports to be a thorough analysis of the research on LGBT identities that just so happens to lend legitimacy to many of the arguments against affirming LGBT people and protecting them under the law.
>
> But the report has no new information, no new arguments, and—despite its 143 pages of analysis—is still more notable for what it doesn't say...
>
> One of its co-authors is Dr. Paul McHugh, the retired Johns Hopkins University professor who is generally the only scientist whom opponents of transgender equality ever cite and who has his own history of overt anti-LGBT bias. The report was published in *The New Atlantis*, a journal that is affiliated with the anti-LGBT Ethics and Public Policy Center and prides itself on not being peer-reviewed. And when it was released on Monday, the Heritage Foundation's Daily Signal was ready to promote the report and the fancy featurette video that accompanies it—one that looks suspiciously like plenty of other Heritage-produced videos.

They then go on to a lengthy debunking of the report.

Anderson frequently points out that Dr. Paul McHugh is a "distinguished" professor at the Johns Hopkins University School of Medicine. So, what do the faculty at Johns Hopkins think of the "study"?

Several distinguished faculty members wrote, in *Hopkins faculty disavow 'troubling' report on gender and sexuality*:[26]

30

As faculty at Johns Hopkins, we are committed to serving the health needs of the LGBTQ community in a manner that is informed by the best available science — a manner that is respectful and inclusive and supports the rights of LGBTQ people to live full and open lives without fear of discrimination or bias based on their sexual orientation or gender identity.

That is why the recent report, released by one current and one former member of our faculty on the topic of LGBTQ health, is so troubling. The report, "Sexuality and Gender: Findings from the Biological and Psychological and Social Sciences," was not published in the scientific literature, where it would have been subject to rigorous peer review prior to publication. It purports to detail the science of this area, but it falls short of being a comprehensive review...

We wish to make clear that there are many people at Hopkins who hold a profound and long-standing commitment to the health, wellness, well-being, and fair and non-stigmatizing treatment of LGBTQ people and communities. We do not believe that the "Sexuality and Gender" report cited above is a comprehensive portrayal of the current science, and we respectfully disassociate ourselves from its findings...

This summer's tragic events in Orlando reminded all of us of the virulence of the oppression of LGBTQ people. We stand with the LGBTQ community, and with their allies, for dignity, inclusion and the recognition that homophobia and transphobia have no place in our institutions. Respect requires no less from all of us.

The authors are all faculty at the Johns Hopkins Bloomberg School of Public Health. Dr. Chris Beyrer is the Desmond Tutu Professor of Public Health and Human Rights. Dr. Robert W. Blum is William S. Gates Sr. Professor and chair of the Department of Population, Family and Reproductive Health; he also served on the

Institute of Medicine Committee on LGBT Health Issues and Research Gaps and Opportunities. Tonia C. Poteat is an assistant professor in the Departments of Epidemiology and International Health. The following Johns Hopkins faculty members also contributed to this article: Danielle German, David Holtgrave, David Jernigan, Michelle Kaufman, Joanne Rosen and Dr. Ron Valdiserri.

Outside of the anti-trans echo chamber, the "study" is nearly universally disavowed. And people are not afraid to stand up to the authors. For instance, Dr. Lauren Beach, the director of LGBTI Research at Vanderbilt, decided she had had enough. She released a letter signed by nearly 600 experts on LGBT health stating that the *New Atlantis* report "does not represent prevailing expert consensus opinion about sexual orientation or gender identity related research or clinical care."[27] We read:

> Beach told The Daily Beast that she and her Vanderbilt colleague Dr. Jesse Ehrenfeld began collecting the signatures "a couple months back" and decided to release the letter after a wave of anti-LGBT bills in 2017 because "we think it's critical that the best scientific evidence is used to inform public policy."...
> "We are writing to the public at large as experts in this area of LGBTI health and we want to send a strong message that peer-review is essential for scientific integrity," Beach told The Daily Beast. "We want to clearly state the *New Atlantis* article is not peer-reviewed and that—as experts— we disagree with the conclusions expressed in the report. They're scientifically and medically unfounded." Among other conclusions, the *New Atlantis* paper cast doubt on the idea that "in order to live happy and flourishing lives, we must somehow discover this innate fact about ourselves that we call sexuality or sexual orientation" and advocated taking "a skeptical view toward the claim that sex-reassignment procedures provide the hoped-for benefits."

The letter and its signatories can be read here.[28]

Anti-Transgender Policy

In part feeling emboldened by Trump's election, anti-transgender activists are pushing bills aimed at harming and ostracizing transgender citizens at a record pace.[29] More than just "bathroom bills," their agendas are becoming more widespread. Some examples are:[30]

- bills that try to prevent trans people from getting transition-related care,
- bills that force trans children out of the restrooms matching their gender at school,
- bills that encourage businesses to discriminate against trans people, and even
- bills making it a crime for parents to support their trans children.

Why is it so important for anti-trans activists to attack transgender citizens and children? Part of it is the "God Hates Fags (and trans people)" attitude by some otherwise good Christians, but more importantly and insidiously is that trans people are being scapegoated. Heather Hogan writes:[31]

> The modern Republican party has *always* needed at least one minority group to scapegoat. Without the ability to create propaganda against a dangerous "other" that is out to destroy families, their power is diminished. Few voters will bypass their own fears and stoked prejudices to examine the actual policies (tax cuts and deregulation, hey!) of the GOP. It seems that even Trump and his cronies have recognized that well-funded, well-organized, politically victorious gay rights activists aren't the minority they want to tangle with,

so instead they want to divide and disorder the LGBT community: you've got Milo over here trying to isolate the T from LGBT and the Moral Majority over there waiting to pounce.

As Polly Anna Rocha pointed out yesterday, these decisions by Trump's administration and state legislators specifically target trans women: "We are the ones that conservatives are daring to call men in dresses, we're the ones that have to face direct physical and systemic violence for living publicly in spite of misconceptions, and yet we're the ones they claim are out to molest and assault unsuspecting (cisgender) women and children, despite there being zero evidence to back this up."

We further read:

Everyone who was paying attention knew it was coming: The Trump administration was always going to go after trans people. His team of soulless, scapegoating, power-grabbing bigots was always going to roll back the basic civil rights trans people finally won under President Obama and wink at state legislatures to go as hard as they want against trans people, economic and social repercussions — like the ones faced by North Carolina after passing HB2 — be damned...

Despite the apparent infighting between DeVos and Jeff Sessions on the issue, the decision to target trans people was an easy political choice for Trump as it's one of the only things that naturally marries his "alt-right Breitbart" supporters and white evangelical Christians still claiming a moral high ground by clinging to the GOP...

The Trump Administration's decision to go after trans people is a happy marriage of policy ideas shaped and espoused by Milo and Duggar. It makes Breitbarters happy. It makes Baptists happy. It makes the lives of trans women and trans kids infinitely more dangerous and terrifying. And it doesn't do a damn thing to protect anyone besides the men who have proven themselves apologists and perpetrators of sexual assault against children, the very crime they claim to want to keep trans women from committing.

Trump's ban on transgender troops is part of this. Jason Wilson writes:[32]

> It wasn't just the substance of the announcement; it was also its motive: in essence, the tweets were a sop to socially conservative legislators who might otherwise have held up his agenda (on this, Politico's report[33] from behind the scene is a must read).
>
> Many conservatives, however, have decided that this is a hill they are prepared to die on. The broad social acceptance of homosexuality, and the legality of same sex marriage, has made the political scapegoating of lesbians, gays and bisexuals tricky. This has put transgender folks in the crossfire of the culture wars, as attested by bathroom bills, ceaseless transphobic vilification in conservative media and now Trump's ban, which, among other things, will put out and serving trans troops in a hideous position.

"I say this with love...

...but not really."

This is an example of the wolf in sheep's clothing. Anti-trans activists often claim the high ground by stating that their hate and discriminatory actions are based on love or compassion. Simply saying so once will magically make all of their abhorrent words and behaviors respectable.

Even Eric Teetsel, author of the Kansas resolution to dehumanize[34] transgender people claims of the resolution, "we are motivated by love."

We are not fooled.

Ryan T. Anderson almost but not quite comes close to claiming "love" for his victims (transgendered people). On page 4 of *When Harry Became Sally*, he writes:

> ...social conservatives (including myself) should take care to be respectful and compassionate toward people we may disagree with.

In Chapter 3, he writes:

> This charge should prompt social conservatives (like myself) to be careful not to attack or marginalize people...

In the conclusion, he writes:

> ...we must be careful not to stigmatize those who are suffering.

In a highly insulting online defense of his alleged "scorn, contempt and belittlement" of transgendered people[35] (in which he claims that "sex reassignment does not adequately address the psychosocial difficulties faced by people who identify as transgender," transitioners face "poor outcomes," repeats the desistence myth, and compares gender dysphoria to anorexia), he writes:

> ...people who experience a gender identity conflict should be treated with respect and civility...
> We need to respect the dignity of people who identify as transgender...

He has thus written: *be respectful; be careful not to attack or marginalize people; be careful not to stigmatize; should be treated with respect and civility;* and *respect the dignity.*

36

Inconceivable. He keeps using those words. I do not think they mean what he thinks they mean. Indeed, we see little of that in the book. What we do see is deliberate and likely malicious misgendering (using terms opposite of someone's gender) and deadnaming (using a transitioned person's old name). On page 10 we read about Chaz:

...Chasitiy Bono, the daughter of Sonny and Cher...

And:

[Laverne] Cox, a man...

On page 11:

...a teenage boy, Jazz Jennings...

Is deliberate misgendering OK or just petty/malicious? In *No, misgendering me is not okay or justifiable. Yes, this is a big deal*, Amelia Gapin elaborates on the following points:[36]

- It is never okay to misgender me
- You don't actually see me as a woman
- You don't respect me as a friend, equal, or person
- You don't care what feelings you trigger for me
- You don't think what you say matters
- You are making light of my transition and what it means to be transgender
- You think my identity is yours to define
- You think it's okay to out me as transgender to a room full of people
- Simply put, gendering me properly *is* a big deal

She concludes:

If you are incapable or unwilling to gender me properly, it tells me a lot about what you think of me and transgender people as a whole. This is a big deal for me and I am not okay with you misgendering me, nor will I listen to your attempts to justify it. It is never okay. Ever.

That is to say, *no, deliberate misgendering is not OK*. It is maliciously disrespecting the dignity of transgendered people. By deliberate misgendering every chance that he gets, Ryan T. Anderson is making a mockery of his "We need to respect the dignity of people who identify as transgender" statement. It appears to me that he means no part of that.

The hate group ACPeds states that they "care for them [LGBT people] with as much compassion and empathy and sound medicine as any other patient."[37] But they spend their careers as anti-LGBT activists.

Tony Perkins of the hate group[38] Family Research Council writes "Children suffering from gender dysphoria deserve our compassion."[39] Yet in the same article insults the trans person in question, misgenders her, and argues against allowing transgender people access to medical care.

Claiming "love" or "compassion" once and then feeling that their egregious attacks against the transgender population are good to go is, to me, malarkey.

Brynn Tannehill wisely puts this as:[40]

"I'm saying this with love..."
People who start conversations with this one remind me of that not-so-bright kid in bootcamp who heard from some guy you could say anything you wanted to the Drill Instructor if you started the sentence, "With all due respect..." You can guess how well that goes over.
To illustrate the concept in reverse: for all the transphobes out there I am saying this with love. You and

your circular family tree are a blight on humanity. If you weren't spewing hate, I suspect you would be squatting in a ditch poking berries up your nose.

Offensive? You bet. It's also every bit as offensive as attacking my identity. If you think you need to start with "I'm saying this with love," then we're all probably better off if you didn't say whatever was going to come afterwards.

CHAPTER THREE

Transitioners Tell Their Stories

In *When Harry Became Sally*, there is no evidence that Ryan T. Anderson reached out to a single transgender person. I know of no evidence that he has ever, in his life, knowingly engaged in a conversation with a transgender person (Walt Heyer does not count, as he is not transgender; he is a vocal opponent of trans rights[1]). This includes the detransitioners in Chapter 3 of his book—he found the stories on the internet and posted excerpts from their stories without asking them. Many were upset at being misrepresented.[2]

Carey posted:[3]

> I was upset to be used as a rhetorical device by someone who does not respect me and other detransitioners enough to contact us, or even alert us that we are being used as rhetorical devices.

Crash wrote:[4]

> I was enraged to see my story distorted and used. I would never have agreed to be included in such a book.

Max added:[5]

> [I] am not okay with it, and the women mentioned are working together right now to figure out our next move.
> I don't personally know any detransitioned women who are on board with anything the Heritage Foundation does.

He posted stories of six people who detransitioned and none of those who did not. That is hardly balanced journalism. It is highly biased. I will feature stories of both people who did transition and those who did not.

Detransitioners...

...Until They Weren't.

Ryan T. Anderson touts Kenneth Zucker's former clinic. Zucker will not allow a child to transition; instead he tries to get them to admit that they are OK with their assigned sex. This sounds like conversion therapy. I will start with one of his patients, as described in his and Bradley's book, *Gender Identity Disorder and Psychosexual Problems in Children and Adolescents*,[6] and relayed by Zinnia Jones's Genderanalysis.net:[7]

> José was initially assessed at age 10 (IQ = 104). Although he [sic] did not meet the full DSM-III criteria for gender identity disorder, he was markedly cross-gender-identified. He had been referred by school authorities because of his effeminacy and the attendant social ostracism that he experienced. His parents, who did not speak English, denied that he had any problems and refused to receive feedback. José was referred again by school authorities at age 13 because of similar concerns. At this time, both José and his parents were more receptive to receiving help, but they did not follow through. When José was seen for an initial follow-up at age 15, he reported no gender dysphoria and an exclusively heterosexual [gynephilic] orientation. He claimed that he had just been elected class president and that he had received A's in his schoolwork; however, he could provide no documentation of these claims. A year later, José requested an interview. At that time, he was cross-dressing and passing socially as a female. He had

dropped out of school and run away from home, and he was abusing recreational drugs and engaging in prostitution. He reported an exclusively homosexual [androphilic] orientation and urgently requested sex reassignment surgery. He stated that in the initial follow-up he had "lied" about his feelings because he had been "embarrassed."

Here, we have a child who was coerced (embarassed) into saying that they were cisgender (and even heterosexual), only to run away from home and worse. That seems like child abuse.

Below is another one of Zucker's patients:[8]

When Trish's son was seven years old, he declared that God had made a mistake and he was meant to be a girl. He had always liked to dress up like his sisters in princess costumes and not shown much interest in traditional boy activities. "God doesn't make mistakes," his mom told him. "You are perfect."

But his parents, who lived in Toronto, were worried about him, and after doing some research, they were referred to Dr. Zucker. They met with him four times, but never brought their son. They felt it wouldn't be a good match, but they were reassured by what Dr. Zucker was telling them: Their son would likely grow up to be gay. Trish, who asked that her family not be identified, says Dr. Zucker told them "it was important to encourage our child to feel more comfortable with the gender matching their biology." At the same time, Trish recalls, "we wanted our son to be a boy. So we jumped at any suggestion. ... When we heard he is probably gay, you can't imagine the relief we felt."

By age 10, however, he was still struggling, so they returned to CAMH; this time, they didn't see Dr. Zucker at the clinic, but went to see another clinician about their son's anxiety. That clinician, they recall, consulted with Dr. Zucker. The advice they received was to normalize male behaviour and reduce female diversions. So they went home and removed the princess costumes and his father tried to interest him in karate.

Their son didn't say much – he didn't forcefully insist he was a girl – and his parents didn't talk to him about it. Based on how they'd interpreted the advice at CAMH, they were worried about putting the idea in his head. But Trish would continue to find clothes hidden away. At night, her son would pull his hair out while he slept. Trish and her husband knew this couldn't go on. At 13, when their son came out as gay, they thought, thankfully, that Dr. Zucker had been right.

A year later, their child told them what she had been feeling for years: She was transgender. This time, her parents took her to Toronto's Hospital for Sick Children, where the truth spilled out and she was given hormone blockers to slow puberty.

She finally told them: "Every birthday, every time I blew out the candles, I wished to be a girl." She admitted to hiding costumes and wigs so she wouldn't get in "trouble," and expressed anger that her parents had not asked her more about how she was feeling, and that they had waited so long to start the hormone treatment.

When at 15, she wanted to start taking estrogen, her mother sat her down. "I said, 'How can I give a 15-year-old, who is not responsible, who doesn't clean their room, who doesn't always tell the truth – how can we give you this power to change your body in an irreversible way for the rest of your life?'"

She recalls her daughter answering back: "This is my entire existence. I can't live this way any more."

Her parents deeply regret that they didn't see this sooner; if they had gone to a psychologist who encouraged them to accept their daughter as she was and follow her lead, Trish believes they could have spared her years of pain.

Her husband agrees: "Every step we make that affirms her femininity, it just gets better and better."

In *More Than Two Developmental Pathways in Children With Gender Dysphoria?* By Steensma & Cohen-Kettenis (2015),[9] again relayed by Zinnia Jones's Genderanalysis.net, we read[10] that of the desisters in their study, five later came back to the clinic. The Genderanalysis.net article concludes:

> Given these reports, it's worth considering whether widespread notions that dysphoric children will become gay adolescents and adults may be harmful to these youth, placing inappropriate pressure on their development and understanding of their gender. It is disconcerting that hypothetical cases of transition regret among trans youth continue to receive outsized attention from the media and the public, even as actual observed cases of regret for *not* transitioning in adolescence appear to be far more common.

ThinkProgress has quite a number of similar stories.[11] I will share just two more:

Olivia

Olivia K. Maynard, a 42-year-old retail makeup saleswoman in Houston, only faintly remembers beginning to understand who she was at around age 4 when she was growing up in Defiance, Ohio. "I don't remember saying I'm a girl; I only remember being me," she told ThinkProgress. "Whatever it was was the very basis of my personality... my manner, my energy, my aura." But as soon as that femininity was perceived by her family, it was interrupted. "I was not allowed to form an identity." She met so much resistance so quickly that she never had the chance to express how persistent, consistent, and insistent her identity was.

Her family actually subjected her to violence and forced her to conform to being a boy. "I wasn't allowed to show emotion, I had to play male-dominated sports, I was forced to get into fights and I had to accept violence for being a sissy," she recalled. "Like random attacks. My family would just attack me." Maynard wasn't even allowed to have female friends. "I compartmentalized myself very rigidly,"

45

she said, finding ways to express her identity only when she was away from her family.

When Maynard was 21, her mother committed suicide, calling her before her death to apologize and to encourage her "to try to be happy," but she just couldn't. "She encouraged me, but I was too repressed." She buried her identity for another 18 years. By all appearances, she fit the desistance myth's expectations perfectly — until she didn't.

Three years ago, Maynard realized she just couldn't repress being trans anymore and had to cope with the dysphoria she'd been experiencing. Transitioning has already made a big difference in her life, and she describes herself as being "in a very blessed situation as far as trans people go." But she knows her entire life would be different if she could have experienced acceptance at a young age. "I can't comprehend what I lost really. I'm glad sometimes that I don't know."

Amanda

Amanda Hunter, a cabinet maker in Ontario, Canada, had a childhood that was a lot like how Jacq Tchoryk thinks his would be if he hadn't been affirmed in his transition. "I stayed home, I stayed alone," she told ThinkProgress. She knew she was trans around age 10, but at age 15, her mom's doctor sent her to the Clarke Institute to receive reparative therapy.

Toronto's Clarke Institute of Psychiatry, later incorporated into the Centre for Addiction and Mental Health (CAMH), ran a Child Gender Identity Clinic that was so notorious for its regressive ex-trans practices that many trans activists nicknamed it "Jurassic Clarke." It was there that researchers like Susan Bradley and Kenneth Zucker conducted their research that still contributes to the desistance myth. CAMH closed in 2015 after an investigation confirmed that reparative therapy — by then banned under Ontario law — was still being performed there.

Hunter has repressed many of the memories from her time at Clarke, though she's been able to recover some medical records of her time there. "Shivering — I shivered a lot when I was there," she recalled. "I wasn't cold; I was terrified. The memories — I try not to think of those memories because they cause a lot of pain. It's hard to explain."

As a result of the therapy, she buried aspects of herself for decades and just tried to blend in. If she'd been part of a study at CAMH, she'd have surely been counted as a desister. But she had anger issues, including a rage that scared even her, and five years ago, "it all came back," she said. "I got to the point in the road where I couldn't go any farther." A therapist started helping her cope and transition, and now, at age 49, she's been "full-time myself" for two years.

"Life is so much better. Friends who've known me for a very long time say it's like I'm a completely different person. I'm outgoing, I'm happy, I'm full of life. Compared to what I once was — I was so shy, quiet, insecure, just everything about me had been crushed during those years." Her workplace respects her identity, she's been in a relationship for over a year, and life is stable and happy. "I wish I could have had this 30 years ago."

The article then states:

These stories demonstrate that kids are coming out as trans at a younger age because society increasingly *allows* them to, not because society is somehow changing them. And though many families are now affirming of their trans kids, stories of gender repression still play out in homes across the country just like they did decades ago for Maynard, Scott, and Hunter — in large part because of the desistance myth.

Despite the prevalence of the desistance myth, there are actually only a few "experts" still promoting the debunked theory. These voices, however, are elevated by conservative echo chambers and are increasingly reaching mainstream audiences, propagating the rejection of transgender kids by distorting, ignoring, or hiding the research that supports affirmation.

Transitioners

I need to go no further than my bookshelves to find happy transitioners, all of whom I have personally met. I have had drinks with most. I know that they are real people and most definitely benefitted from transitioning. Their stories and books are well worth reading and are available online and in many book stores. I would like to quote a lot from these books, but wish to remain within the fair use doctrine, so, feel free to buy the books to continue reading. They are real stories of real transitioners and thus valuable for learning about transgendered people.

Jennifer

Jennifer Finney Boylan is an English professor and acclaimed author. She documented her transition in *She's Not There: A Life in Two Genders*, available at Amazon.[12] Jennifer is a humorous person and enjoyably outspoken.

Not understanding that transsexuality was actually a thing, Jennifer nonetheless imagined herself as a girl:

> Sometimes I played a game in the woods called "girl planet." In it, I was an astronaut who had crashed on an uninhabited world...The thing was, though, that anyone who breathed the air on the planet turned into a girl. There was nothing that you could do about it, it just happened. My clothes turned into a girl's clothes, too, which should give an indication of exactly how powerful the atmosphere was. *It changed your clothes!* Once female, I walked through the cobblestone woods, past the abandoned houses, until I arrived at Governor Earle's mansion, which I started to try

to fix up. It took years, but eventually I had a nice little place put together. By the time astronauts from planet Earth came to rescue me, I had grown into a mature woman...My rescuers would say, "We're looking for James Finney Boylan, the novelist. We found his rocket all smashed up back there in the woods. Do you know where he is, ma'am?"

"I'm sorry," I said. "He's gone now."

She writes that at that age and time, she had not heard the term transsexual, and that "transgendered" had not been invented. That made her understanding of who she really was perplexing. She continues:

But even if I had known the right definitions for these words, I am not sure if it would have made much of a difference to me. Even now, a discussion of transgendered people frequently resembles nothing so much as a conversation about *aliens*. Do you think that there really *are* transgendered people? Has the government known about them for years and kept the whole business secret?

...Although my understanding of exactly how much trouble I was in grew more specific over time, as a child I surely understood enough about my condition to know it was something I'd better keep private. By intuition I was certain that the thing I knew to be true was something others would find both impossible and hilarious.

What she seems to mean is that she may have felt as if she were the only one like that on the planet. This is actually common among transgendered people who have not heard of other transgendered people or had not heard that their condition is real and not that uncommon.

Once a patient understands that they are not alone, and that their condition can be treated if that is what is best for them, a decision may be made to either transition or address their condition in another way.

Transitioning can be daunting and scary. But for some, it feels more of a life or death issue, and they do undergo

49

the difficulties, and blossom. To quote Anaïs Nin, *The day came when the risk to remain tight in a bud was more painful than the risk it took to blossom.*

When one does go out as their true gender for the first few times, it can be frightening. What might people think? Will someone become violent, Or worse?

Jennifer discusses a time going out as herself:

> For one thing, now that I lived alone, I was living as a woman about half of the time. I'd come home and *go female* and pay the bills and write and watch television, and then I'd go back to boy mode and teach my classes. I didn't venture out into the world much *en femme*, although I did get out now and then. It was unbelievably frightening. The first time I ever went outside wearing a skirt and a knit top, I thought I was going to perish from fear. The world felt raw and intimidating; the cold wind howled on my bare legs.
>
> I got as far as an Esso station, where I filled up my tank at the self-serve pump. I waited in line to pay for the gas, and no one looked at me twice. "Thank you, ma'am," said the attendant.
>
> Then I drove home.
>
> I lived in constant fear of detection and kept waiting for the chair of the program to call me up and say, *Boylan, we've heard stories. I hope you understand the consequences.*

Hormone therapy can help one look more like their true gender and "pass" as a member of said sex. Jennifer took estrogen and an anti-androgen. She describes them as, "Well, the one pill makes you want to talk about relationships and eat salad. The other pill makes you *dislike* the Three Stooges."

She eventually transitioned and wrote to her colleagues about her new name and pronouns. And that is the big moment. Once you let the cat out of the bag and tell people at work, it is done. The first day can be scary, but you have done it.

Jennifer kept her position at the college, and she now lives as herself with her family. What I see in many of these stories is that transition could be scary, but the patient does so anyway, as the best option, and in the end, it was the right decision, and the patients' lives greatly improve.

Jamison

I knew who Jamison Green was for many years, and respected him. I first met him at a conference in 2005. It happened that he had some copies of a book that he had just published with him. I was eager to read it, so I got a copy and read it as soon as I got home. It is not just about his transition, but also about trans history and issues. It is *Becoming a Visible Man* and is available on Amazon.[13]

Like many trans kids, he acted more like the sex of which their gender identity aligns. And that can cause trouble with people who expect children to abide by more rigid gender stereotypes. He writes:

> When I was in the fourth grade, just nine years old, I was instructed to leave my regular classroom for an hour two days a week for a special reading session—at least that was how it was presented to me. Twice a week I entered a room with a female speech therapist and several other children with real speech impediments. My problem was that someone had determined that my voice was too low, and that my speech patterns were not appropriate to my assigned gender...
>
> After several weeks of increasing tension between the speech therapist and me, school officials recommended I be taken to a throat specialist. Dutifully, my mother made an appointment and took me to see a man whose office was like a dentist's, but instead of a drill next to the chair, there was a small gas flame. The doctor would use the flame to heat his little mirror, which was a lot like the one the dentist used. Then he would grab my tongue with a coarse paper towel

and pull it, hard, and stick the hot mirror in my throat. The heat kept it from fogging up, so he could examine my vocal cords. Mom and I made at least three visits to this man's torture chamber, after which he told my mother he could do surgery on my vocal cords that would give me a fifty percent chance of having a soprano voice. He implied that this would result in more people reflecting femininity back to me when I spoke. Only then did I realize all this was about making me into a girl. I was relieved when my mother said, "No thank you." This was nothing compared to what happens to many other gender-variant children (Burke, 1996; Scholinski, 1997).

Dr. Jamison Green is mentioning Daphne Scholinski. Her harrowing memoir, *The Last Time I Wore a Dress*,[14] describes her devastating three-year ordeal with conversion therapy. She spent those three years, from age 15 to 18, in mental institutions. Characterized as "an inappropriate female," she underwent therapy aimed to act more like a girl. One million dollars of insurance money was spent in this attempt. When the money ran out, she was let go.

Jamison transitioned as an adult and does make one heck of an awesome guy. For the past several years, he has been a trans advocate and is a member of several medical and legal groups.

Donna

I first learned who she was in 2003 when I watched a Learning Channel documentary with the sensationalist title of *The Sex Change Capital of the World*. In it, Donna Rose supported her friend Elizabeth when Elizabeth had Facial Feminization Surgery (FFS) by Dr. Douglas Ousterhout. Thus, I recognized Donna and Elizabeth at a conference the following year. Donna had undergone FFS herself earlier. Both women looked awesome.

In her 2005 *Wrapped in Blue,* available on Amazon.[15] Donna recounts her "Journey of Discovery." I found the story to be a difficult but determined journey with hardships but an eventual happy ending. Having gender dysphoria can be very difficult, but can be overcome by transitioning. The transition can be the most difficult thing a person ever does, but it is often necessary.

She described the awkward time of "coming out" to someone as trans. Here, she did so to her sister over the phone, after her sister got an idea that there was something important to learn. She writes:

> "Are you gay?" she asked.
> "No," I replied, amused that she would ask.
> "Are you an alcoholic?"
> "Nope."
> "Are you cheating on Elizabeth?"
> "Of course not!"
> "Is it sexual?"
> "No, not really."
> "Porn?"
> "NO!"
> "Is it health related?"
> "No. I'm fine. Really!"
> "You'll *never* guess," I told her. "It's something I have been dealing with for my entire life, and I'm just now facing it. It's crushing Elizabeth."
> She continued to guess, and I continued to deny. Until she got too close to home.
> "Are you a transvestite?" she eventually asked.
> After a second, I responded. "No. But you are getting close now."
> And with that, I explained it all to her.

She states that she had been dealing with all of her life. But it came to a point where she had to address it.

53

Donna had to work this through with her wife, Elizabeth (not the same Elizabeth who had FFS in the documentary), and her son. And at her workplace.

Donna had been an athlete and had a rugged, handsome face. That can make things harder for a transgendered woman. People may be more inclined to be disrespectful or worse when they see a woman that they perceive might not be cisgendered. An expensive and painful remedy is Facial Feminization Surgery (FFS).

Donna went to Dr. Douglas Ousterhout in San Francisco (the same as her friend did).

She has several before and after photos in her book. The transformation is amazing. No makeup needed; she is a beautiful woman.

Such a surgery can be lifesaving. I have met many of Dr. Ousterhout's patients, many whose lives he has helped in such a fundamental way. But it is expensive, and many cannot afford it.

Donna still needed to come out at work and legally change her gender. But she succeeded. She also had Sex Reassignment Surgery (gender affirming surgery). Her life is better after successfully addressing gender dysphoria. At the end of the book, she writes:

I have no regrets. I was content. I felt loved, and peaceful, and over the next several months I continued to become comfortable in my new routine. I took joy in the simple firsts that I found confronting me every day: my first visit to the woman's restroom at a Buffalo Bills game, my first time swimming in a woman's bathing suit...my first birthday where I didn't need to wish that this would be my last one as a boy. In those simple firsts and simple pleasures I found the joy that had eluded me for so many years, and that so many people seem to take for granted: the simple peace that comes from being comfortable in your own skin.

Samantha

Samantha's book, *Through the Jungle: A Traveler's Guide*,[16] is written, in part, in the form of a diary. She kept a diary throughout transition and from it, we can precariously live the life of someone as they transition. A brief quote from the book is:

> Had I been born like the majority of people on the planet, I would have been raised to fit my assigned gender...yet nature is not always perfect, and what appears on the outside does not always match the inside. I would find that out at the age of four, when I realized I just didn't feel like the boy I was told, and looked down at myself, I was supposed to be. This is typical of most transgender people, I would find out many years later. I have spoken to many who can pinpoint a part of childhood when they realized that the gender role assigned to them didn't fit, and at the ripe age of four, I too knew I just wasn't a boy.

What we have read in this chapter are stories of people who were transgendered as children, but prevented from transitioning via conversion therapy. But that did not work. It only harmed them.

We also read stories of people who were transgendered as children and finally transitioned as adults. They did not desist. They were trans as kids and grew up to be trans as adults. All transitioned and all are far more happy because of it.

CHAPTER FOUR

What Makes Us Harry or Sally? (or in between)

This chapter is about gender identity. Most people have a gender identity that corresponds to the sex that they were assigned at birth. This assignment also generally corresponds to their karyotype of having XX or XY chromosomes. But numerous exceptions do occur.

Gender identity, sexual orientation, and karyotype align in most cases. But there are a percentage of people with whom these do not, and it is not their "fault" or "choice"; it is simply the way that they were born.

Both gender identity and sexual orientation are mental—they reside in the brain. What causes an anatomic male to have a sexual orientation towards men (a sexual orientation towards men is known as *androphilic*) rather than towards women (a sexual orientation towards women is known as *gynephilic*), or vice versa for women, is not yet known, and may have several causes.

It is the same with gender identity, and gender identity is a very strong force in one's life.

Sex, intersexuality, sexual orientation, and gender identity run on a spectrum. Some men are more or less masculine than others. Some people's genitals fit more of the ideal male or female paragons of genitalia, some less. Secondary sex characteristics (such as breasts, facial and body hair, an Adam's apple, etc.) are mixed as well. They generally fit the paradigm, but some men have breasts and some women have facial and body hair, for example.

Karyotypes vary as well. In most cases, one has XX or XY chromosomes. One might state, "If you have a Y chromosome, then you are male; if you have two X chromosomes, then you are female." But this does not always fit. About 1 out of 500 males assigned at birth have XXY karyotypes (known as Klinefelter syndrome).[1] Thus, they have both "a Y chromosome" and "two X chromosomes." XXXY and XXXXY karyotypes also exist.[2]

One can have one X chromosome and nothing else. This is known as Turner Syndrome.[3] This occurs in about 1 out of 2,500 female births.[4] The karyotype is labeled Xo.

In Swyner Syndrome,[5] an anatomic female is born, but has an XY karyotype, and usually has a female gender identity. The person may never know of the condition. If she has a karyotype performed and learns that she is XY, should laws force her out of the women's room based on her genetics? I would argue against it. Let her pee in peace.

Likewise, people born male can have an XX karyotype.[6] They may not know it unless a karyotype is performed. Which restroom should he use? Some activists would ban him from the boys' room. This makes no good sense to me.

Just as some people have a sexual orientation for their own sex (homosexual), or the other (heterosexual), or to both (bi), or none at all (asexual, which occurs in about 1% of the population[7]), Some people have a gender identity that conforms to their sex assigned at birth (cisgender), and some have a gender identity that is that of the opposite sex (transsexual, or transgender), some have gender identities that are a mix of the two or to neither (genderqueer, or nonbinary).

Frequency

It would seem optimal for the gender identity to match natal sex, but this simply does not always occur. The

58

Williams Institute recently ran a large survey in all 50 states to determine the percentage of individuals who identify as transgender. They found that it was about 0.6% of the population.[8]

Etiology

How does this occur? Is it inborn? What causes the brain to have a transgender identity? Is it environmental or genetic? Are there differences between cisgender and transgender brains? I will examine all of these.

Inborn

Anti-transgender activists sometimes declare that gender identity is a choice. But it is not. For those with a binary gender identity (cisgender or transgender), the identity is inborn and generally strong. It is evident at a very early age. A recent study by Brenda K. Todd, et al. found:[9]

> From an early age, most children choose to play with toys typed to their own gender. In order to identify variables that predict toy preference, we conducted a meta-analysis of observational studies of the free selection of toys by boys and girls aged between 1 and 8 years...We found that boys played with male-typed toys more than girls did (Cohen's d = 1.03, p < .0001) and girls played with female-typed toys more than boys did (Cohen's d = −0.91, p < .0001).

They stated, "Gender differences in toy choice exist and appear to be the product of both innate and social forces."

This occurs not only in humans, but other primates as well. A 2008 study[10] by Janice M. Hassett, et al. found similar behavior in rhesus monkeys.

A study by Gerianne M Alexander and Melissa Hines found similar behavior in vervet monkeys.[11]

Both studies suggested that exposure to prenatal hormones can affect such behavior. This leads to the hypothesis that prenatal hormones can affect one's gender identity.

Before exploring that, I would like to show an example where a cisgender person was raised as the opposite sex, with the idea that nurture, rather than nature, was responsible for gender identity.

As described in John Colapinto's *As nature made him: the boy who was raised as a girl*,[12] In the late 1960s, psychologist John Money tested his hypothesis that if a child were brought up in a certain gender role, the child would develop the identity of that gender.

His infamous twins experiment started after Bruce Reimer lost his penis as a baby during a botched circumcision in 1966. His twin brother, Brian, had a normal circumcision. Dr. Money persuaded the parents to have Brian undergo a sex change operation and be raised as a girl, named Brenda. He would work with and observe the twins to prove his hypothesis, that gender identity developed primarily as a result of social learning from early childhood and that it could be changed with the appropriate behavioral interventions.

However, "Brenda" never developed a female gender identity. He transitioned to a male gender role by age 15 and used the name David Reimer. In 2004, at the age of 38, he ended his own life by shooting himself in the head with a sawed-off shotgun.

As with David, attempts to socially condition (impose) a gender on an individual are generally ineffectual and can be harmful. In *Discordant Sexual Identity in Some Genetic Males with Cloacal Exstrophy Assigned to Female Sex at Birth*,[13] William G. Reiner, M.D. and John

60

P. Gearhart, M.D. examined the patients years later. They found:

> We assessed all 16 genetic males in our cloacal-exstrophy clinic at the ages of 5 to 16 years. Fourteen underwent neonatal assignment to female sex socially, legally, and surgically; the parents of the remaining two refused to do so. Detailed questionnaires extensively evaluated the development of sexual role and identity, as defined by the subjects' persistent declarations of their sex.
>
> Eight of the 14 subjects assigned to female sex declared themselves male during the course of this study, whereas the 2 raised as males remained male. Subjects could be grouped according to their stated sexual identity. Five subjects were living as females; three were living with unclear sexual identity, although two of the three had declared themselves male; and eight were living as males, six of whom had reassigned themselves to male sex. All 16 subjects had moderate-to-marked interests and attitudes that were considered typical of males.

Thus, the patients had inborn male gender identities and forcing them into a female identity can backfire. Most of the 14 assigned female at birth transitioned by the time of the study. All acted typically male. This is the same as with transgendered people. They retain their inborn gender identity and attempts to force them into the role assigned to them at birth does not change their inborn gender identities.

These studies help to show that gender identity is innate. We also have seen that about 0.6% of the population is transgender, having the gender identity different than the sex assigned at birth. In many cases, the best treatment for such people is transitioning to the gender role that fits their identity.

Work done by Ai-MinBao and Dick F.Swaab shows:[14]

During the intrauterine period a testosterone surge masculinizes the fetal brain, whereas the absence of such a surge results in a feminine brain. As sexual differentiation of the brain takes place at a much later stage in development than sexual differentiation of the genitals, these two processes can be influenced independently of each other.

Their research highlighted the following:

- Gender identity and sexual orientation are permanently programmed in the fetal brain.
- Testosterone in the fetal stage determines sexual differentiation of the human brain.
- The degree of genital masculinization does not necessarily reflect that of the brain.
- No evidence indicates social environment affects gender identity or sexual orientation.
- Sex differences in the brain determine sex-specific prevalence of brain disorders.

Prenatal androgens not only affects gender identity, but also other tangible physiology. Prenatal androgens have been linked to the ratio of the length of the second and fourth digits (2D:4D) in humans and other animals. One would expect, then, that gender identity and finger length ratios to correlate in FtM patients. And in many cases, they do.

The 2017 study, *The Biologic Basis of Transgender Identity: 2d:4d Finger Length Ratios Implicate a Role For Prenatal Androgen Activity*, which examined 155 people, states:[15]

Our findings are consistent with a biologic basis for transgender identity and the possibilities that FTM gender identity is affected by prenatal androgen activity.

The 2014 study, *Finger length ratios in Serbian transsexuals*, states:[17]

> FMT [female-to-male transsexuals] showed the lowest 2D:4D of the left hand when compared to the control males and females. Results of our study go in favour of the biological aetiology of transsexualism

Even a study in which Kenneth Zucker participated agrees. The 2008 study, 2D:4D finger-length ratios in children and adults with gender identity disorder, states:[17]

> ...women with GID [meaning FtM transmen] had a significantly more masculinized ratio compared to the control women. This last finding was consistent with the prediction that a variance in prenatal hormone exposure contributes to a departure from a sex-typical gender identity in women.

So, how does the situation of a prenatal brain developing to that of a transgender one occur?

Genetic Causes

One study in *Biologic Psychiatry*[18] examined androgen receptor genes, stating, "There is a likely genetic component to transsexualism, and genes involved in sex steroidogenesis are good candidates. We explored the specific hypothesis that male-to-female transsexualism is associated with gene variants responsible for undermasculinization and/or feminization. Specifically, we assessed the role of disease-associated repeat length polymorphisms in the androgen receptor (AR), estrogen receptor β (ERβ), and aromatase (CYP19) genes."

They found a correlation in the AR gene. They state, "A significant association was identified between transsexualism and the AR allele, with transsexuals having longer AR repeat lengths than non-transsexual male control subjects (p = .04)."

They concluded, "This study provides evidence that male gender identity might be partly mediated through the androgen receptor."

Recently, as reported in The Times[19] (and elsewhere[20]) that, "they have identified genetic variants that may play a role in gender identity, giving backing to gender dysphoria having a physical basis."

The article states:

> ...researchers have identified a panel of genes, including DNA involved in the development of nerve cells and the manufacture of sex hormones, that could provide a biological basis for gender dysphoria. The findings add to the growing evidence that transgender people have fundamental differences in their brains and biochemistry that may help to explain why they feel at odds with their birth sex. "It lends legitimacy, if that needs to be added, that transgender is not a choice but a way of being," Ricki Lewis, a geneticist and author of textbooks, said. "I think people will be excited by this."

For female-to-male transsexuals, we read, in *A polymorphism of the CYP17 gene related to sex steroid metabolism is associated with female-to-male but not male-to-female transsexualism:*[21]

> CYP17 −34 T>C SNP allele frequencies were statistically significantly different between FtM transsexuals and female controls (CYP17 T: 55/98 [56%] and CYP17 C: 43/98 [44%] versus CYP17 T: 1253/1826 [69%] and CYP17 C: 573/1826 [31%], respectively). In accordance, genotype distributions were also different between FtM transsexuals and female controls using a recessive genotype model (CYP17 T/T+T/C: 39/49 [80%] and C/C 10/49 [20%] vs. CYP17 T/T+T/C:

821/913 [90%] and C/C 92/913 [10%], respectively). The CYP17 −34 T>C allele and genotype distributions were not statistically significantly different between MtF transsexuals and male controls. Of note, the CYP17 −34 T>C allele distribution was gender-specific among controls (CYP17 C: males; 604 of 1512 [40%] vs. females; 573 of 1826 [31%]). The MtF transsexuals had an allele distribution equivalent to male controls, whereas FtM transsexuals did not follow the gender-specific allele distribution of female controls but rather had an allele distribution equivalent to MtF transsexuals and male controls.

They concluded, "These data support CYP17 as a candidate gene of FtM transsexualism and indicate that loss of a female-specific CYP17 T −34C allele distribution pattern is associated with FtM transsexualism."

Another gene, CYP21A2, shows correlation to gender dysphoria. In *The Journal of Clinical Endocrinology & Metabolism*, Stephen M. Rosenthal reports that "studies in 46,XX patients with "classical" congenital adrenal hyperplasia (CAH) caused by mutations in CYP21A2, resulting in 21-hydroxylase deficiency and varying degrees of genital masculinization, demonstrate a greater than expected number of patients with gender dysphoria, 'atypical gender identity,' or who were transgender."[22]

J. Cortés-Cortés et al., in their study, *Genotypes and Haplotypes of the Estrogen Receptor a Gene (ESR1) Are Associated With Female-to-Male Gender Dysphoria*, found that "XbaI-rs9340799 is involved in FtM gender dysphoria in adults. Our findings suggest different genetic programs for gender dysphoria in men and women."[23]

R. Fernández et al. found something similar.[24] They report:

There is an association between the ERβ gene and FtM transsexualism. Our data support the finding that ERβ function is directly proportional to the size of the analyzed polymorphism, so a greater number of repeats implies greater transcription activation, possibly by increasing the function of the complex hormone ERβ receptor and thereby encouraging less feminization or a defeminization of the female brain and behavior."

Fu Yang et al. found that a specific mutation that affects the RYR3 protein correlates to Gender Dysphoria. They report, "Importantly, protein structure modeling of the RYR3 mutations indicated that the R1518H mutation made a large structural change in the RYR3 protein. Overall, our results provide information about the genetic basis of GD."[25]

Twin studies were done as well. The study by FL Coolidge et al. entitled *The heritability of gender identity disorder in a child and adolescent twin sample,* concluded "Overall, the results support the hypothesis that there is a strong heritable component to GID [Gender Identity Disorder]. The findings may also imply that gender identity may be much less a matter of choice and much more a matter of biology."[26]

Milton Diamond also examined twins for Gender Identity Disorder concordance, and found similar results.[27]

Environmental

Diethylstilbestrol (DES) is a synthetic form of the female hormone estrogen. It was prescribed to pregnant women between 1940 and 1971 to prevent miscarriage, premature labor, and related complications of pregnancy.[28]

The medication, as the report continued, was shown not to be effective for those complications. However, it was linked to cervix and uterine cancers in females born to women who used the drug. Prescriptions to pregnant women ceased.

Dr. Scott Kerlin noted that prenatal exposure to DES could affect male babies as well. He began examining this in 1999 and started the DES Sons International Network.

I recall perusing that internet group in the early days and I, as well as others, noted that many of the "DES sons" had female names. So, someone asked the obvious question, "why?"

The answer appears that, since many of the natal males in the group who were exposed prenatally to the synthetic estrogen, DES, they had a female gender identity and had transitioned to a female gender role.

This was examined further in various studies, including *Prenatal DiEthylStilbestrol Exposure in Males and Gender-related Disorders*.[29]

It stated:

1. Among the population of DES sons joining the network who have discussed a history of gender identity concerns, personal stories and/or introductions have been received from more than 150 individuals with either confirmed or "strongly suspected" DES exposure.

2. Responses were received from at least 93 individuals with confirmed prenatal DES exposure who self-identify as either transsexual (male-to-female), transgendered (male-to-female), "gender dysphoric," or intersex. The distribution of these 93 individuals is as follows:

67

Confirmed DES-Exposed and Gender-Related Issues

	(N=93)
(1) Confirmed Exposed and Transsexual:	54 individuals
(2) Confirmed Exposed and Transgender:	26 Individuals
(3) Confirmed Exposed and Gender Dysphoric:	10 individuals
(4) Confirmed Exposed and Intersex:	3 individuals

3. There have been at least 65 individuals with "strongly suspected but not yet confirmed" exposure who indicated they are either either transsexual (male-to-female), transgendered (male-to-female), "gender dysphoric," or intersex. The distribution of these 65 individuals is as follows:

Strongly suspected, not confirmed DES Exposed and Gender-Related Issues

	(N=65)
(1) Suspected Exposure and Transsexual:	36 individuals
(2) Suspected Exposure and Transgender:	22 Individuals
(3) Suspected Exposure and Gender Dysphoric:	7 individuals
(4) Suspected Exposure and Intersex:	None reported

The pool of DES exposed or suspected exposed was approximately 500 participants (60% confirmed and 40% suspected). While the gender-related issues nomenclatures were different, we normally put "transsexual", "transgender", and "gender dysphoric" together under the transgender umbrella. And 153 out of about 500 is about 30% of the population in the pool that either were or suspected of having prenatal exposure to DES were transgender. In general, only about 0.6% of the population is transgender. This shows a strong correlation between prenatal exposure to DES and being born transgender.

DES is a known endocrine disruptor. Endocrine disruptors are chemicals that may interfere with the body's endocrine system and produce adverse developmental, reproductive, neurological, and immune effects in both humans and wildlife. A wide range of substances, both natural and man-made, are thought to cause endocrine disruption.[30]

Endocrine disruptors can mimic or partly mimic naturally occurring hormones in the body like estrogens (the female sex hormones), androgens (the male sex hormones), and thyroid hormones, potentially producing overstimulation. They can bind to a receptor within a cell and block the endogenous hormone from binding. The normal signal then fails to occur and the body fails to respond properly. Examples of chemicals that block or antagonize hormones are anti-estrogens and anti-androgens.[31]

Studies on how these can affect gender behavior of children have been done, including one by Zana Percy, et al.[32]

They state, "Phthalates, used in a variety of consumer products, are a group of chemicals that are ubiquitous in the environment, and their metabolites are detectable in most humans. Some phthalates have anti-androgenic properties; a prior study reported an association between gestational exposure to phthalates and reduced masculine behaviors in preschool boys."

They measured phthalates in pregnant women's urine and followed up when the children were eight years old to examine gender-related behavior. They found that "higher maternal mono-isobutyl phthalate (MiBP) concentrations were associated with higher odds of membership in the least typical play behaviors group for males (OR = 1.69, CI = 1.00–2.86)."

And concluded that "increased urinary MiBP concentrations were associated with less masculine gender-related play behaviors in males."

They explained:

> Play behaviors, which are an accepted method to determine gender identity in children, are a critical factor in diagnosing Gender Dysphoria, according to the American Psychiatric Association. In humans, androgens contribute to sexually-dimorphic brain and genital development, especially during late first trimester and early second trimester gestation. Sexually-dimorphic behaviors include toy preference, play style, and visual-spatial abilities. Higher testosterone levels during pregnancy have been associated with more masculine play behaviors in both boys and girls [21], suggesting that hormonal changes in the fetal environment can have effects on brain development.

DES may have been a major cause of Baby Boomers presenting as transgender. Other endocrine disruptors may contribute to the apparent rise in younger transgender patients.

Chemicals ingested by pregnant women, either intentionally or from the environment, can and do cause gender-related changes in the brains of the developing fetus. Many are born transgender. It is not their fault. Yet the present anti-transgender movement insists that they are crazy, refuse to affirm their identities, and try to prevent them from obtaining medical care. That is pure cruelty.

It's all in the mind. Or, rather, the Brain

The brains of men and women do have statistical differences. Transgender brains fit more with the brains of

70

the sex that fits their gender identities. We see that in a number of ways.

In 1999, in the Journal of Neuroscience, Ruben C. Gur et al. examined sex differences in brain gray and white matter in healthy young adults.[33]

They found noticeable differences, and confirmed that women have a higher percentage of gray matter, whereas men have a higher percentage of white matter.

In 2009, Eileen Luders et al. examined the regional gray matter in transwomen (male-to-female, or MTF). They found that "MTF transsexuals show a significantly larger volume of regional gray matter in the right putamen compared to men. These findings provide new evidence that transsexualism is associated with distinct cerebral pattern, which supports the assumption that brain anatomy plays a role in gender identity."[34]

Studies were done on female-to-male transsexuals. In the *Journal of Psychiatric Research*, Giuseppina Rametti et al. examined the brains of FtM patients prior to hormone therapy, and concluded that, "Our results show that the white matter microstructure pattern in untreated FtM transsexuals is closer to the pattern of subjects who share their gender identity (males) than those who share their biological sex (females). Our results provide evidence for an inherent difference in the brain structure of FtM transsexuals."[35]

In 1995, in the journal *Nature*, J.-N. Zhou et al. examined one region of the brain, the bed nucleus of the stria terminalis (BSTc), which is "essential to sexual behavior" and is larger in men than in women, and found that MtF transsexuals had a female-sized BSTc size. They report, "A female-sized BSTc was found in male-to-female transsexuals. The size of the BSTc was not influenced by

71

sex hormones in adulthood and was independent of sexual orientation."[36]

A larger study was done by FP Kruijver et al. in 2000.[37] This time, they counted the number of neurons rather than measuring the size. They found:

> Transsexuals experience themselves as being of the opposite sex, despite having the biological characteristics of one sex. A crucial question resulting from a previous brain study in male-to-female transsexuals was whether the reported difference according to gender identity in the central part of the bed nucleus of the stria terminalis (BSTc) was based on a neuronal difference in the BSTc itself or just a reflection of a difference in vasoactive intestinal polypeptide innervation from the amygdala, which was used as a marker. Therefore, we determined in 42 subjects the number of somatostatin-expressing neurons in the BSTc in relation to sex, sexual orientation, gender identity, and past or present hormonal status. Regardless of sexual orientation, men had almost twice as many somatostatin neurons as women ($P < 0.006$). The number of neurons in the BSTc of male-to-female transsexuals was similar to that of the females ($P = 0.83$). In contrast, the neuron number of a female-to-male transsexual was found to be in the male range. Hormone treatment or sex hormone level variations in adulthood did not seem to have influenced BSTc neuron numbers. The present findings of somatostatin neuronal sex differences in the BSTc and its sex reversal in the transsexual brain clearly support the paradigm that in transsexuals, sexual differentiation of the brain and genitals may go into opposite directions and point to a neurobiological basis of gender identity disorder.

Although some people have a gender identity that is not binary, most people do have a hard and fast gender identity. And for them, it cannot be changed. Dr. Jamison

Green sums this up in his book, *Becoming a Visible Man*. He writes:[38]

> Any transsexual person can tell you that no matter how much social pressure is applied, one's gender identity can't be changed by forced social performance. Oprah asked Colapinto "What was for you, John, the most disturbing thing you uncovered while doing this?" (That is, while researching his book about Reimer's childhood.) Colapinto replied, "I think the most disturbing thing was the image of a child trying to get the world to hear who he really was, and the effort to try to make psychologists and psychiatrists understand what he was feeling, and his inability to do so. That's extremely disturbing." The same effort to express who they really are is common to transsexual people who don't share Reimer's horrific circumstances. What Colapinto uncovered was his own ability to empathize with someone whose identity is denied.

A task at hand is getting people to empathize with the transgender population. Their gender identity is real and cannot be changed. Efforts to coerce them into changing their brain structure by conversion therapy or by social pressures and laws will not be effective. Often, what is effective is social transition, hormone therapy, and sometimes, surgery.

This will now be discussed.

CHAPTER FIVE

Gender Identity and Affirmation Surgery

It takes courage to grow up and become who you really are. - e. e. cummings

Gender Dysphoria may develop in any fetus. It is not yet known all of which causes the gender of a developing brain to mismatch their natal sex, although much has already been discussed—there appears to be several ways that this can occur. Very often, the gender identity is strong and lifelong. This can lead to severe distress for transgendered people. Unfortunately, some people find it difficult to sympathize with such people. A survey done on transgender suicide attempt rate found it to be frighteningly high (41% overall).[1]

This tragic statistic is in part due to hostile and bigoted reactions by people who are anti-transgender. The survey stated that the rates for each of the following:

- Family chose not to speak/spend time with them
- Discrimination, victimization, or violence at school, at work, and when accessing health care
- Harassed or bullied at school or work
- Doctor or health care provider refused to treat them
- Suffered physical or sexual violence at work or school
- Discrimination, victimization, or violence by law enforcement

Were all above 50%. This is not acceptable in a polite society.

Standards of Care

What is the best methods to treat those with Gender Dysphoria? This is one of the tasks of the World Professional Association for Transgender Health (WPATH). They are responsible for the standards of care (SoC)[2] for transgender and gender nonconforming people. The SoC is presently in Version 7, but Version 8 may be out later this year.

Ryan T. Anderson and anti-transgender activists often argue against medical treatment for transgender patients. Some argue instead for harmful and ineffective reparative therapy. Often, their arguments are based on religion, pseudoscience, opinion, sheer animus, or blind faith, and do not seek to help transgender people. Often, their arguments are used for creating laws that directly harm the transgender population, including legalizing discrimination and keeping them out of public facilities. In contrast, the WPATH SoC is based on science. The SoC states:

> One of the main functions of WPATH is to promote the highest standards of health care for individuals through the articulation of Standards of Care (SOC) for the Health of Transsexual, Transgender, and Gender Nonconforming People. The SOC are based on the best available science and expert professional consensus...
> The overall goal of the SOC is to provide clinical guidance for health professionals to assist transsexual, transgender, and gender nonconforming people with safe and effective pathways to achieving lasting personal comfort with their gendered selves, in order to maximize their overall health, psychological well-being, and self-

fulfillment. This assistance may include primary care, gynecologic and urologic care, reproductive options, voice and communication therapy, mental health services (e.g., assessment, counseling, psychotherapy), and hormonal and surgical treatments. While this is primarily a document for health professionals, the SOC may also be used by individuals, their families, and social institutions to understand how they can assist with promoting optimal health for members of this diverse population.

WPATH realizes that treatments can vary. What is best for one patient may be different from another patient. They recognize a difference between gender nonconforming and gender dysphoria. The SoC further states:

Gender nonconformity refers to the extent to which a person's gender identity, role, or expression differs from the cultural norms prescribed for people of a particular sex. Gender dysphoria refers to discomfort or distress that is caused by a discrepancy between a person's gender identity and that person's sex assigned at birth (and the associated gender role and/or primary and secondary sex characteristics). Only some gender nonconforming people experience gender dysphoria at some point in their lives.

Treatment is available to assist people with such distress to explore their gender identity and find a gender role that is comfortable for them. Treatment is individualized: What helps one person alleviate gender dysphoria might be very different from what helps another person. This process may or may not involve a change in gender expression or body modifications. Medical treatment options include, for example, feminization or masculinization of the body through hormone therapy and/or surgery, which are effective in alleviating gender dysphoria and are medically necessary for many people. Gender identities and expressions are diverse, and hormones and surgery are just two of many options available to assist people with achieving comfort with self and identity.

Gender dysphoria can in large part be alleviated through treatment. Hence, while transsexual, transgender, and gender nonconforming people may experience gender dysphoria at some point in their lives, many individuals who receive treatment will find a gender role and expression that is comfortable for them, even if these differ from those associated with their sex assigned at birth, or from prevailing gender norms and expectations.

Psychotherapy is a main part of WPATH therapy. So too is trying what behavior is optimal for alleviating dysphoria. This can include cross-dressing either at home or at certain public places. I have attended many transgender conferences in the past two decades. At each one, there are many adults, frequently male assigned at birth, that attend and dress as women just for the conference and sometimes at home. Often, they come with their spouses. At their workplaces, their gender roles are those that align with their sex assigned at birth. No hormones or surgery needed. And this is effective for some patients.

Some live as their true selves at home, but as the gender of their birth-assigned sex at work.

For some, this is not enough. The SoC allows for physical interventions, including hormone therapy and surgeries. But these are not taken lightly. There have been inappropriate candidates that do end up with surgery, such as Walt Heyer, who later detransitioned.

The SoC seeks to prevent that. Letters of recommendation from qualified professionals are required for hormone therapy and for surgery. Genital surgery requires two letters, as well as completion of living at least one year in the gender role that fits the sex to which their surgery will allow them to resemble.

Hormone therapy

The content for a letter for hormone therapy is described in the SoC as such:

The recommended content of the referral letter for feminizing/masculinizing hormone therapy is as follows:

1. The client's general identifying characteristics;
2. Results of the client's psychosocial assessment, including any diagnoses;
3. The duration of the referring health professional's relationship with the client, including the type of evaluation and therapy or counseling to date;
4. An explanation that the criteria for hormone therapy have been met, and a brief description of the clinical rationale for supporting the client's request for hormone therapy;
5. A statement about the fact that informed consent has been obtained from the patient;
6. A statement that the referring health professional is available for coordination of care and welcomes a phone call to establish this.

The SoC criteria for hormone therapy are:

1. Persistent, well-documented gender dysphoria;
2. Capacity to make a fully informed decision and to consent for treatment;
3. Age of majority in a given country (if younger, follow the Standards of Care outlined in section VI);
4. If significant medical or mental health concerns are present, they must be reasonably well-controlled.

The physical effects of hormone therapy:

Feminizing/masculinizing hormone therapy will induce physical changes that are more congruent with a patient's gender identity.

• In FtM patients, the following physical changes are expected to occur: deepened voice, clitoral enlargement (variable), growth in facial and body hair, cessation of menses, atrophy of breast tissue, increased libido, and decreased percentage of body fat compared to muscle mass.
• In MtF patients, the following physical changes are expected to occur: breast growth (variable), decreased libido and erections, decreased testicular size, and increased percentage of body fact compared to muscle mass.

Genital surgery

This is not for everyone. The SoC states:

Sex Reassignment Surgery Is Effective and Medically Necessary

Surgery – particularly genital surgery – is often the last and the most considered step in the treatment process for gender dysphoria. While many transsexual, transgender, and gender nonconforming individuals find comfort with their gender identity, role, and expression without surgery, for many others surgery is essential and medically necessary to alleviate their gender dysphoria. For the latter group, relief from gender dysphoria cannot be achieved without modification of their primary and/or secondary sex characteristics to establish greater congruence with their gender identity. Moreover, surgery can help patients feel more at ease in the presence of sex partners or in venues such as physicians' offices, swimming pools, or health clubs. In some settings, surgery might reduce risk of harm in the event of arrest or search by police or other authorities.

The SoC criteria for genital surgery are:

Criteria for metoidioplasty or phalloplasty in FtM patients and for vaginoplasty in MtF patients:

1. Persistent, well documented gender dysphoria;
2. Capacity to make a fully informed decision and to consent for treatment;
3. Age of majority in a given country;
4. If significant medical or mental health concerns are present, they must be well controlled;
5. 12 continuous months of hormone therapy as appropriate to the patient's gender goals (unless the patient has a medical contraindication or is otherwise unable or unwilling to take hormones).
6. 12 continuous months of living in a gender role that is congruent with their gender identity;

Psychological outcomes

In Ryan T. Anderson's, *When Harry Became Sally* book, we read "the most beneficial therapies focus on helping people accept themselves and live in harmony with their bodies."[3] That sounds a lot like reparative therapy/conversion therapy to me. But the main point is that he seems to be making is that hormone therapy and surgery should be denied to the patient. He bolsters his claim by posting some detransition stories from people whom he had never met or even contacted.[4]

Is transitioning as horrible as he claims? What do actual studies say on this issue?

The 2006 study by G. De Cuypere et al. entitled *Long-term follow-up: Psychosocial outcome of Belgian transsexuals after sex reassignment surgery*,[5] examined 107 Dutch-speaking transsexuals who had undergone SRS between 1986 and 2001, 62 (35 male-to-females and 27 female-to-males). We read:

Socially our subjects had experienced a positive change. A Wilcoxon signed ranks test showed that both the male-to-females ($P= 0.001$) and the female-to-males ($P< 0.001$) were significantly more satisfied with their social relationships than they had been before SRS...Most of our male-to-females (88.6%) and female-to-males (85.2%) felt happy to very happy after surgery. The regret rate was low: only one male-to-female regretted the treatment occasionally, but she went on living as a woman nevertheless. She had had psychotic periods before SRS (axis I diagnosis: delusional disorder—erotomanic type) and scored very low on credibility. A female-to-male who ex-pressed feelings of regret, subsequently requested masculine hormone treatment. At the time of the interview, he was emotionally troubled by a break-up with his girlfriend. Intensive psychotherapy provided him with some stability.

Further, it mentions that the suicide attempt-rate dropped significantly from 29.3% to 5.1%.

In 2015, Ulrike Ruppin and Friedemann Pfäfflin, did a study entitled *Long-Term Follow-Up of Adults with Gender Identity Disorder*.[6] We read, "The aim of this study was to re-examine individuals with gender identity disorder after as long a period of time as possible. To meet the inclusion criterion, the legal recognition of participants' gender change via a legal name change had to date back at least 10 years. The sample comprised 71 participants (35 MtF and 36 FtM). The follow-up period was 10–24 years with a mean of 13.8 years."
The results were:

Positive and desired changes were determined by all of the instruments: Participants reported high degrees of well-being and a good social integration. Very few participants were unemployed, most of them had a steady relationship, and they were also satisfied with their relationships with family and friends. Their overall evaluation of the treatment process for sex reassignment and its effectiveness in reducing gender dysphoria was positive. Regarding the results of the standardized questionnaires, participants showed significantly fewer psychological problems and interpersonal difficulties as well as a strongly increased life satisfaction at follow-up than at the time of the initial consultation.

In a press release from the European Association of Urology,[7] we read that "A team at the University hospital in Essen, Germany, led by Dr. Jochen Hess, followed 156 patients for a median of more than 6 years after surgery. They developed and validated the new Essen Transgender Quality of Life Inventory, which is the first methodology to specifically consider transgender QoL."
They concluded:

> They found that there was a high overall level of satisfaction with the outcomes of surgery. When comparing the QoL of the last four weeks with the QoL during the time of publicly identifying as transgendered there was a highly significant increase on all subscales of the ETL as well as for the global score indicating a large improvement of QoL in the course of the transitioning process.

Doctor Hess commented:

> The good news is that we found that around three-quarters of patients showed a better quality of life after surgery. 80% perceived themselves to be women, and another 16% felt that they were 'rather female'. 3 women in 4 were able to have orgasms after reassignment surgery.

When asked about regrets, only 2 percent of respondents in a survey of transgender people in the UK had major regrets regarding the physical changes they had made, compared with 65 percent of non-transgender people in the UK who have had plastic surgery.

On page 2 of When Harry Became Sally, Ryan T. Anderson writes:

And never mind that "transitioning" treatment has not been shown to reduce the extraordinary high rate of suicide attempts among people who identify as transgender...In fact, people who have had transition surgery are nineteen times more likely than average to die by suicide.

This is quite misleading. It reads as if transitioning increases the suicide rate. That is the opposite of what is true.

He references a study by Dhejne et al. entitled Long-Term Follow-Up of Transsexual Persons Undergoing Sex Reassignment Surgery: Cohort Study in Sweden.[8]

He does so again on page 73. Again, reading as if Dhene's study concludes that transitioning *makes patients suicidal.* That is not what the report states. Anderson appears to be misrepresenting the study, and misrepresenting on purpose. The study actually states:

For the purpose of evaluating whether sex reassignment is an effective treatment for gender dysphoria, it is reasonable to compare reported gender dysphoria pre and post treatment. Such studies have been conducted either prospectively or retrospectively, and suggest that *sex reassignment of transsexual persons improves quality of life and gender dysphoria.* (emphasis added)

Cristan Williams discussed such misrepresentation with Cecilia Dhejne.[9] We read:

WILLIAMS: Before I contacted you for this interview, were you aware of the way your work was being misrepresented?

DHEJNE: Yes! It's very frustrating! I've even seen professors use my work to support ridiculous claims. I've often had to respond myself by commenting on articles, speaking with journalists, and talking about this problem at conferences. The Huffington Post wrote an article about the way my research is misrepresented. At the same time, I know of instances where ethical researchers and clinicians have used this study to expand and improve access to trans health care and impact systems of anti-trans oppression.

Of course trans medical and psychological care is efficacious. A 2010 meta-analysis confirmed by studies thereafter show that medical gender confirming interventions reduces gender dysphoria. (emphasis added)

The interview continues:

DHEJNE: People who misuse the study always omit the fact that the study clearly states that it is not an evaluation of gender dysphoria treatment. If we look[10] at the literature,[11] we find[12] that several[13] recent studies[14] conclude that WPATH Standards of Care compliant treatment decrease gender dysphoria[15] and improves mental health.[16]

The same Dhejne (et al.) did a study on 767 people who applied for legal and surgical sex reassignment in Sweden between 1960 and 2010. They concluded:[17]

There were 15 (5 MF and 10 MF) regret applications corresponding to a 2.2 % regret rate for both sexes. There was a significant decline of regrets over the time period.

A 2.2% regret rate.

Dr. Anderson's insistence that transition leads to "tragic outcomes" is highly misleading. It is generally beneficial to those with gender dysphoria.

In the 2015 study, *Long-Term Follow-Up of Adults with Gender Identity Disorder*, we read:[18]

The follow-up period was 10–24 years with a mean of 13.8 years...Positive and desired changes were determined by all of the instruments: Participants reported high degrees of well-being and a good social integration. Very few participants were unemployed, most of them had a steady relationship, and they were also satisfied with their relationships with family and friends. Their overall evaluation of the treatment process for sex reassignment and its effectiveness in reducing gender dysphoria was positive. Regarding the results of the standardized questionnaires, participants showed significantly fewer psychological problems and interpersonal difficulties as well as a strongly increased life satisfaction at follow-up than at the time of the initial consultation.

In the 2014 study, *Effects of sex reassignment surgery on quality of life and mental health in transsexuals*, we read:[19]

The SRS used in the treatment of transsexuality releases the conflict and makes the transformation on official gender and is associated with improvements in quality of life, self esteem, family support, sexual life satisfaction and interpersonal relationships and reduction in worries about gender discrimination and gender victimization.

A recent large review of 56 studies ties it all up. The Cornell University review on the well-being of transgender people states:[20]

We conducted a systematic literature review of all peer-reviewed articles published in English between 1991 and June 2017 that assess the effect of gender transition on transgender well-being. We identified 56 studies that consist of primary research on this topic, of which 52 (93%) found that gender transition improves the overall well-being of transgender people, while 4 (7%) report mixed or null findings. We found no studies concluding that gender transition causes overall harm. As an added resource, we separately include 17 additional studies that consist of literature reviews and practitioner guidelines.

We further read, in Endocrine Today's article *Gender transition positively affects well-being of transgender adults*:[21]

> ...the research indicated high overall well-being and mental health status among participants who transitioned, with 0.3% to 3.8% of participants indicating regret. "Regrets following gender transition are extremely rare and have become even rarer as both surgical techniques and social support have improved," the researchers wrote in the study summary online.

That is, the overwhelming majority of studies showed improvement in well-being, and none showed negative outcomes. Regret was rare.

In *When Harry Became Sally*, we read, "the most beneficial therapies focus on helping people accept themselves and live in harmony with their bodies."[22] But he gives no alternatives to medical care besides conversion therapy, nor does he back up that opinion with science. Science clearly shows that transition and surgery give favorable outcomes.

We see no reason for medical care to be denied to transgender people who would benefit from it. Indeed, WPATH states that trans medical treatment is a medical necessity,[23] and further that insurance should cover the required treatments.

Denying medical treatment is not "compassionate." It is cruel. It can lead to suicides. Allowing medical treatment can and does alleviate the dysphoria and let people live normal and happy lives.

> *Don't hide yourself in regret*
> *Just love yourself and you're set*
> – Lady Gaga, in *Born This Way*

CHAPTER SIX

Childhood Dysphoria and Persistence

Many people who have transitioned say that they knew that their gender did not fit their assigned sex as early as they can remember.[1] And many seriously wish that they were able to start as a child. The pain caused by having to undergo the puberty that did not match their identity lingers on—they can be less "passable" and can more easily be identified as trans, leading to discrimination, injury, and even murder. These statistics may get worse if the anti-transgender activists get their way and turn more otherwise good citizens against the trans minority.

Desisters vs. Persisters

On age 84 of *When Harry Became Sally*, Ryan T. Anderson writes:

> We know that differences between the sexes begin in the womb, and they are manifested in our behavior from infancy...These results cannot be explained away by reference to cultural stereotypes or the social pressures that operate among humans.
>
> It's also difficult to blame socialization for the differences in how newborn babies respond to objects and to people...This pattern of behavior in the first day of life indicates that "we come out of the box with some cognitive sex differences built in."

And that is an important point. We have already seen that male and female brains do differ, and that the brains of transgender patients have pertinent structures more in line with the brains of the sex of which they identify—gender identity is built in. They are "born that way."

At the start of Chapter 6 in *When Harry Became Sally*, Ryan T. Anderson relates a story in the Washington Post entitled *Transgender at Five*.[2] It is about a transgender boy named Tyler, who, as early as two-years-old *insisted* that he was a boy.

That is the key. As discussed, gender identity is inborn. Persisters quite often insist that they really *are* the "opposite" sex.

A girl might be a tomboy, but grow up to be happy about being a woman and may marry a man. She was never a boy or transgender in the first place. She should not count as a desister.

Boys can be gentle and like hanging out with girls. That does not make them transgender or a desister if they grow up to be a happy man.

We should understand that some children are gender variant or gender nonconforming, and accept that. We should also understand and accept that some children have the gender identities of the "opposite" sex and *insist* that they are indeed the gender that they say that they are. They grow up to retain that identity, and may be best served by allowing an early transition. These are the persisters.

Many practitioners are already differentiation between gender-variant children and transgender kids in order to better serve all of them. Dr. Johanna Olson-Kennedy, who works at Children's Hospital Los Angeles, said that sometimes interviews with new gender-questioning clients reveal, pretty quickly, that they aren't trans. "And it's clear, it's clear," she said. "I think that once you see hundreds and hundreds of kids you get a feeling for kids that are and kids that aren't."[3]

Dr. Diane Ehrensaft, director of Mental Health and founding member of the Child and Adolescent Gender Center in San Francisco, notes that the *way* children express this can also offer valuable clues: There's a meaningful distinction between a natal (biologically male) boy saying "I *am* a girl" as opposed to "I *wish* I were a girl."[4]

Michelle Cretella, president of the hate group[5] "American College of Pediatricians" counters with, "the repeated behavior of impersonating a girl alters the structure and function of the boy's brain in some way— potentially in a way that will make identity alignment with his biologic sex less likely."[6]

To quote a colleague, *that is utter horse shit.* Donning a dress does not turn a cisgendered kid into a transgendered kid. Cisgender and Transgender people are born that way.

Success from Proper Diagnosis

It is important to differentiate between gender variant non-transgender patients (which end up being labeled desisters) and insisters (persisters). The key is that if a child is "insistent, persistent, and consistent" in signaling over an extended period that they were assigned the wrong gender at birth, that's a strong indication they're transgender.

An important modification was made in the DSM-V criteria for gender dysphoria (previously known as "gender identity disorder," or GID). The criteria now require the strong desire to be or insistence that they are the other sex. In the DSM-IV, the insistence was just one of the options.[7]

This means that in the old criteria, children with gender variant behavior could be diagnosed as having GID even though they were not (not insistent).

An alternative set of criteria, the ICD-10 *Classification of Mental and Behavioural Disorders: Clinical Descriptions and Diagnostic Guidelines,* also require "persistent and intense distress" about being their natal sex or "insisting" that they are the other sex.[8]

Following these or similar guidelines will decrease desistence rates. In 2013, Thomas D. Steensma et al. did a study entitled *Factors Associated with Desistence and Persistence of Childhood Gender Dysphoria: A Quantitative Follow-Up Study.*D Their study consisted of 127 adolescents (79 boys, 48 girls), who were referred for GD in childhood (<12 years of age) and followed up in adolescence. They found:

> We found a link between the intensity of GD in childhood and persistence of GD, as well as a higher probability of persistence among natal girls. Psychological functioning and the quality of peer relations did not predict the persistence of childhood GD. Formerly nonsignificant (age at childhood assessment) and unstudied factors (a cognitive and/or affective cross-gender identification and a social role transition) were associated with the persistence of childhood GD, and varied among natal boys and girls.

They concluded that: "Intensity of early GD appears to be an important predictor of persistence of GD."

On page 136 of *When Harry Met Sally,* Ryan T. Anderson quotes Zucker on some of his patients.[9] We read:

> [W]hen asked why he wanted to be a girl, one 7-year-old boy said that it was because he did not like to sweat and only boys sweat. He also commented that he wanted to be a girl because he liked to read and that girls read better than boys.

An 8-year-old boy commented that "girls are treated better than boys by their parents" and that "the teacher only yells at the boys." His view was that, if he was a girl, then his parents would be nicer to him and that he would get into less trouble at school.

These children are obviously not gender dysphoric and would not be classified as such. They are not even gender variant or gender nonconforming. They wanted to be the other sex out for reasons of taking an advantage.

Yet Anderson, in discussing these patients, concludes, "Had they been brought to a different clinic—like the typical gender clinic today—their parents might have been counseled to initiate a social transition and then put these children on puberty blockers."

No, Dr. Anderson. Just, no.

Please read the WPATH Standards of Care and the DSM-5 criteria. Responsible caretakers do not put children without a GID or Gender Dysphoria diagnosis on puberty blockers. *Nor do they subject any child to conversion therapy.*

It seems to me that he may be trying to stir fears that trans advocates will kidnap little children and force them into sex changes. That is NOT how it works.

What works, again, is proper diagnosis. Persisters, by and large, are trans and should be allowed medical treatment. We will see further evidence of how this is effective when we discuss actual desistence rates.

The Desistance Myth

On page 2 of When Harry Became Sally, Ryan T. Anderson stated, "the best studies of gender dysphoria...show that between 80 and 95 percent of children who express a discordant gender identity will come to identify with their bodily sex if natural development is allowed to proceed."

He repeats this bold claim on pages 36-37, 119, 123, and 125. What are these "best studies"? In the endnotes, these lead to his answer—a single document, an amicus brief (I would call it an *animus* brief) by Paul McHugh, Paul Hruz, and Lawrence Mayer (some very biased anti-transgender activists) for the Supreme Court case *Gloucester County School Board v. G.G.*, in which a transgendered boy, Gavin Grimm, wanted to pee in peace at his school. As one may imagine, the three anti-trans activists were against that idea.

Among other ugly things that they wrote against transgender people in the brief was the statistic that Dr. Anderson so frequently quotes:

"All competent authorities agree that between 80 and 95 percent of children who say that they are transgender naturally come to accept their sex and to enjoy emotional health by late adolescence."

What "competent authorities" agree with that? His statistic appears to be merely his opinion.

In *The shoddy roots of the desistance myth* section of *The pernicious junk science stalking trans kids: The 'desistance' myth doesn't explain why transgender children are thriving*,[10] ThinkProgress examines how these faulty statistics came to be. We read:

Dating back decades, there are about a dozen studies that prop up the desistance myth. Each claims to have studied a cohort of kids with GID and found that a significant percentage (around 60 to 90 percent) of those kids ended up "desisting" in their gender dysphoria and embracing the gender that they were assigned at birth. Even the most recent of these studies, however, relied upon the older DSM-

IV diagnostic criteria, and that's just the beginning of their flaws.

In their 2016 book *Raising the Transgender Child*, Dr. Michele Angello and Alisa Bowman break down the main problems with the research into three main concerns. First, the studies included children who simply were not transgender. Several also concluded that participants desisted simply because they did not complete the study. Moreover — especially given these first two flaws — the sample sizes of actual transgender kids were incredibly small (with most including fewer than five).

Kristina Olson, an associate professor of psychology at the University of Washington, is pioneering a new wave of research about transgender kids that aims to avoid these pitfalls, and as such, she's also been one of the most outspoken critics of the conclusions drawn from desistance studies. In a 2016 critique published in the *Journal of the American Academy of Child & Adolescent Psychiatry*, she explained succinctly, "[C]lose inspection of these studies suggests that most children in these studies were not transgender to begin with."

For example, in two of the studies, "[w]hen directly asked what their gender is, more than 90% of children with GID in these clinics reported an answer that aligned with their natal sex, the clearest evidence that most did not see themselves as transgender." Essentially, a tomboyish girl would say she still identified as a girl, but would be counted as transgender in the study.

In an interview with ThinkProgress, Olson further expounded on how weak the standard was for assessing which children to include in many of these studies. "A very significant number of kids, 30 to 40 percent, didn't even meet the criteria for GID," she explained. "Even if you thought they met that criteria, which is already less strong than the current criteria, you're still looking at kids that didn't meet the criteria."

Colt Keo-Meier, a clinical child psychologist based in Houston who specializes in gender identity issues, summed up the desistance research to ThinkProgress thusly: "When they were older, of course they didn't transition because they weren't transgender to start with."

Actual Desistance Rates

First, one should define what we consider to be a desister. A tomboy who grows up to be a happy woman is not a desister, for example. She was never transgender.

If we, like Anderson, use a court document, we read in *Re: Kevin [2017] FamCAFC 258 in the Family Court of Australia,* "the case stated records as a fact that 96 per cent of patients treated for gender dysphoria at the Royal Children's Hospital continue to identify as transgender into late adolescence."[11]

That means a 4% desistance rate.

In *Factors Associated with Desistence and Persistence of Childhood Gender Dysphoria: A Quantitative Follow-up Study,*[12] Thomas D. Steensma et al. examined the correlation between persistence and the degree of gender dysphoria. Their study sample consisted of 127 adolescents (79 boys, 48 girls) initially selected. The follow-up had 47 persisters and 46 "desisters".

They then correlated these patients with measures of gender dysphoria scores. They utilized the Gender Identity Interview for Adolescents and Adults (GIIAA) and Utrecht Gender Dysphoria Scale (UGDS). These scores showed very high differences between the groups ($p < 0.001$).

A GIIAA score of below 3.0 indicates gender dysphoria. A UGDS score of above 40.0 indicates gender dysphoria.

The average GIIAA score for persisters was 2.56, and for desisters, 4.33. The average UGDS score for persistent boys and girls were 52.22 and 53.79 respectively, and for desisters, 13.48 and 23.00 respectively.

For the GIIAA criteria for gender dysphoria, 87.2% of the persisters met the criteria and 0% of the desisters. For UGDS, 97.9% of the persisters met the criteria for gender dysphoria and 2.2% (one bisexual natal girl) of the desisters did.

Using proper diagnoses, we have 0% or 2.2% desistance, depending on the criteria used for testing. We also have a near precision result that the 46 "desisters" did not even have gender dysphoria by these criteria.

The Anti-Trans Activists' "Treatment" Plan

On page 211 of When Harry Became Sally, Ryan T. Anderson states that "we need to create a network of clinicians who are ready to help those with gender dysphoria in ways that don't endorse transgender ideology or aim to change people's bodies."

What?! Doctors that do not agree with the ideology of their patients? Will the trans patients be forced into such "help"? And I assume that "or aim to change people's bodies" means denial of medical care. That is just cruel.

He continues with "A network of good doctors and therapists across the nation needs to be assembled, with the primary goal of helping people find healthy alternatives to transitioning, so that they may feel comfortable in their own skin."

There are no "healthy alternatives" that I have heard suggested with the exception of conversion therapy (also known as reparative therapy).

Joseph Nicolosi, a proponent of conversion therapy and the founder of the anti-LGBT[13] group, National Association for Research and Therapy of Homosexuality (NARTH), describes it as such:

The client has come to the therapist seeking assistance to reduce something distressing to him, and the RT psychotherapist agrees to share his professional experience and education to help the client meet his own goal. The therapist enters into a collaborative relationship, agreeing to work with the client to reduce his unwanted attractions and explore his heterosexual potential...But no outcome can be guaranteed.

Kenneth Zucker, who practiced this on children, describes his approach as:[14]

When treatment is recommended, it might include the following: a) weekly individual play psychotherapy for the child; b) weekly parent counseling or psychotherapy; c) parent-guided interventions in the naturalistic environment; and d) when required for other psychiatric problems in the child, psychotropic medication...

If the parents are clear in their desire to have their child feel more comfortable in their own skin, that is, they would like to reduce their child's desire to be of the other gender, the therapeutic approach is organized around this goal.

Let us look at some examples.

Bradley

Bradley was one of Zucker's patients. We read:[15]

Bradley had always had a preference for girls' things. From his earliest days he had chosen girls' dolls, identified with female characters and gravitated toward female children. But Carol had never thought to care. As far as she was concerned, it wasn't a loaded gun; it wasn't a lit cigarette. She says it had really never crossed her mind to say, "I'd really rather you played with a truck."

Carol did not worry too much until one day, Bradley came home bloodied from apparent bullying:

Carol decided to seek professional help. Bradley's school referred her to a psychologist in Toronto named Dr. Ken Zucker, who is considered an expert in gender identity issues. After several months of evaluation, Zucker came back with a diagnosis. Bradley, he said, had what Zucker called gender identity disorder...

Whenever Zucker encounters a child younger than 10 with gender identity disorder, he tries to make the child comfortable with the sex he or she was born with.

So, to treat Bradley, Zucker explained to Carol that she and her husband would have to radically change their parenting. Bradley would no longer be allowed to spend time with girls. He would no longer be allowed to play with girlish toys or pretend that he was a female character. Zucker said that all of these activities were dangerous to a kid with gender identity disorder. He explained that unless Carol and her husband helped the child to change his behavior, as Bradley grew older, he likely would be rejected by both peer groups. Boys would find his feminine interests unappealing. Girls would want more boyish boys. Bradley would be an outcast.

Carol resolved to do her best. Still, these were huge changes. By the time Bradley started therapy he was almost 6 years old, and Carol had a house full of Barbie dolls and Polly Pockets. She now had to remove them. To cushion the blow, she didn't take the toys away all at once; she told Bradley that he could choose one or two toys a day.

"In the beginning, he didn't really care, because he'd picked stuff he didn't play with," Carol says. "But then it really got down to the last few."

As his pile of toys dwindled, Carol realized Bradley was hoarding. She would find female action figures stashed between couch pillows. Rainbow unicorns were hidden in the back of Bradley's closet. Bradley seemed at a loss, she said. They gave him male toys, but he chose not to play at all.

After several months of therapy, things get worse:

> In particular, there is one typically girl thing — now banned — that her son absolutely cannot resist.
>
> "He really struggles with the color pink. He really struggles with the color pink. He can't even really look at pink," Carol says. "He's like an addict. He's like, 'Mommy, don't take me there! Close my eyes! Cover my eyes! I can't see that stuff; it's all pink!'"...
>
> "I mean, he tells us now that he doesn't dream anymore that he's a girl. So, we're happy with that. He's still a bit defensive if we ask him, 'Do you want to be a girl?' He's like 'No, NO! I'm happy being a boy. ...' He gives us that sort of stock answer. ... I still think we're at the stage where he feels he's leading a double life," she says. "... I'm still quite certain that he is with the girls all the time at school, and so he knows to behave one way at school, and then when he comes home, there's a different set of expectations."

It would appear that Bradley may transition when she gets away from her parents. But the abuse she suffered from the conversion therapy may be long-lasting.

Kirk

Kirk is another conversion therapy patient; this time by George Reckers. Kirk's mother relates the story:[16]

> "Well, I was becoming a little concerned, I guess, when he was playing with dolls and stuff," she said. "Playing with the girls' toys, and probably picking up little effeminate, well, like stroking the hair, the long hair and stuff. It just bothered me that maybe he was picking up maybe too many feminine traits." She said it bothered her because she wanted Kirk to grow up and have "a normal life."
>
> Then Kaytee Murphy saw a psychologist on local television.

"He was naming all of these things; 'If your son is doing five of these 10 things, does he prefer to play with girls' toys instead of boys' toys?' Just things like this," she said.

The doctor was on TV that day, recruiting boys for a government-funded program at the University of California, Los Angeles.

"Well, him being the expert, I thought, maybe I should take Kirk in," said Kaytee Murphy. "In other words, nip it in the bud, before it got started any further."

At one table Kirk could choose between what were considered masculine toys like plastic guns and handcuffs, and what were meant to be feminine toys like dolls and a play crib. At the other table, Kirk could choose between boys' clothing and a toy electric razor or items like dress-up jewelry and a wig.

According to the case study, Kaytee Murphy was told to ignore her son when he played with feminine toys and compliment him when he played with masculine toys.

"They pretty much told him he wasn't right the way that he was, but they never really explained it to him what the issue was. They did it through play," Maris said.

Kirk's abuse got worse:

At home, the punishment for feminine behavior would become more severe. The therapists instructed Kirk's parents to use poker chips as a system of rewards and punishments.

According to Rekers' case study, blue chips were given for masculine behavior and would bring rewards, such as candy. But the red chips, given for effeminate behavior, resulted in "physical punishment by spanking from the father."...

During one particularly harsh punishment, their mother recalls, her husband "spanked" Kirk "so hard that he had welts up and down his back and on his buttocks."

She remembers her son Mark saying, "Cry harder, and he won't hit so hard." She says, "Today, it would be abuse."

Sometimes Mark would try to protect his brother, to make his beatings less severe.

"I took some of the red chips and I put them on my side," said Mark, as tears came to his eyes. But he said the beatings were still frequent.

"It left Kirk just totally stricken with the belief that he was broken, that he was different from everybody else," she recalled. "He even ate his lunch in the boy's bathroom for three years of his high school career, if you want to call it that."

Kirk later took his own life. He is another "statistic" of high suicide rates that anti-trans activists brag about. But his suicide was not due to being trans, but (IMHO), due to conversion therapy.

Cincinnati Teen

In one recent case, a teen was saved from such therapy by the courts. He was allowed to stay with his grandparents rather than his parents. We learn:[17]

"'When I was home, dad chased me around the house,'" the grandparents' attorney, Jeffrey Cutcher, quoted the teen as saying. "'When I was home, I lived in terror in that home.'" Cutcher said the trans teen's goal now is to graduate, begin living fulltime as a male, and attend college...

For Cincinnati teen, his parents' rejection was so awful, he emailed a crisis hotline last year and reported that one of his parents had told him to kill himself. They also refused to let him get therapy unless it was Christian-based. The teen said he was forced to listen to Bible scriptures for more than six hours at a time, according to court documents.

That's when Hamilton County Job and Family Services intervened.

In doing so, county advocates appear to have either prevented, or at least postponed, the 17-year old's exposure to further harm through "conversion therapy."

The article concludes:

> The latest Williams Institute report makes a dire prediction for youth like him: "20,000 LGBTQ youths currently between the ages of 13 and 17 will be subjected to conversion therapy from a licensed health care professional before they turn 18. An additional 57,000 will be subjected to the controversial practice from a religious or spiritual adviser before age 18."

The Cincinnati teen was able to escape what we can certainly call child abuse. Certainly, even Ryan T. Anderson would support that. But, NO! He wrote an article blasting the teen's salvation from child abuse.

"Without commenting on the specifics of this case," he wrote.[18] And, without discussing the actual situation or the child abuse *at all*, he went into a lengthy screed against medical therapy for transgender patients, with absolutely no concern that the child was abused and that that was why he was removed from his parents.

On page 212 of When Harry Became Sally, Ryan T. Anderson states, "Religious leaders can contribute to these efforts in various ways. They'll need to provide pastoral care to people struggling with their gender identity."

We have just read that an additional 57,000 will be subjected to the controversial practice from a religious or spiritual adviser before age 18. Let us look at one of these cases.

Carl

He was encouraged to be honest to his parents, but doing so landed him in conversion therapy. He writes at length about his experience in *A Firsthand Account of the Torture of 'Conversion' Therapy*. A few excerpts are:[19]

> The "therapist," Michael, was an older, pale-faced man with graying brown hair. His office was painted sky blue and decorated with white-framed pictures of his family sitting on hay bales, grinning at the camera. The white-on-blue color scheme gave the room the impression of somewhere bright and cheery — a sharp contrast to the concrete, windowless reality of the oppressive space.
>
> "When did your 'best friend' first touch you?" was the first complete sentence Michael ever said to me, his voice full of obvious contempt and disdain.
>
> After the initial shock of being asked such a question passed, I burst into tears. When I eventually looked up from between my hands, I was greeted by Michael's smug face looking gleefully pleased that my gender and sexuality fit neatly into the narrative he had devised.
>
> "She never touched me," I said, gritting my teeth through my tears.

Carl's therapy went on for eight months. Each week, he would descend the dark staircase to be "treated" by Michael:

> I remember the first time Michael slammed his fist down on his desk and screamed:
>
> "You are not gay! You will burn in hell! Jesus died so that you can repent from your sins!"
>
> Too shocked to look away, I made eye contact, and even now I can see his desperate, watery eyes trying to burn those thoughts into my teenage brain, to force them into my psyche.

While Michael paced around the room gesturing, screaming, reciting Bible verses, and even crying, I focused on geometric shapes on the walls, traced the edges of bookcases and file cabinets with my eyes to their intersecting points. The precision and consistency of this exercise was comforting, and allowed me to tune out the chaos around me. I memorized the sound of Michael's wall clock so I could know how much time was left in each "session" without looking; he yelled louder when I looked at the clock...

Eventually I just sat there, listened to him yell at me, and tried to block him out.

My silence angered Michael. He tried different ways of asking me the same questions, and when that didn't elicit a response he would attack my gender expression, my appearance. He was terrifyingly prescient:

> "Why can't you dress more like a lady? Who taught you to dress like this? You see my daughters, they look like women. I can't even tell if you're a girl or a boy. How are you going to ever date a man when you don't even wear makeup? You think Jesus wants you to be a dyke? You think Jesus died so you can march down the street with all your faggot friends?"

...I was totally isolated. I couldn't tell my friends, and the adults I thought I could trust sided with my parents and refused to listen when I tried to explain what was happening to me. I was alone with Michael each week for what felt like an eternity. I could feel my life slowing to a crawl that I thought might never end during those hours in that cold basement office.

It wasn't until years later, after coming out as a transgender man, that I began to understand the hell I was put through. It wasn't until I learned about the foundational work of my friend and colleague Sam Ames with the #BornPerfect campaign[20] at the National Center for Lesbian Rights that I could contextualize the excruciating hours I spent with Michael as abuse aimed at "fixing me."

Across this country, LGBT youth are subjected to terrifying sessions with pastors and therapists where they are force-fed toxic messages that they are intrinsically broken. Youth look to parents, faith, and community for guidance navigating the already bumpy road to self-realization, and internalize these messages and carry them into adulthood. For those of us "lucky" enough to make it out alive, it can take years to understand that you can't repair what isn't broken.

He concludes, "I am not broken. LGBT youth are not broken. We were all #BornPerfect."

And let us not forget Leelah Alcorn, who took her own life after her parents refused to affirm her but instead subjected her to conversion therapy. Fallon Fox, who survived conversion therapy, writes, in *Leelah Alcorn's Suicide: Conversion Therapy Is Child Abuse*:[21]

In a suicide note posted, but since deleted, from her Tumblr, Leelah wrote that when she told her mom about being transgender, her mother "reacted extremely negatively, telling me that it was a phase, that I would never truly be a girl, that God doesn't make mistakes." Leelah wrote that she was subsequently taken to Christian therapists, who reinforced the notion that being transgender was "wrong."

...If you know anything about the very real state of having gender dysphoria, you know that telling him or her it is wrong is one of the worst things in the world a transgender person can hear. It deepens the depression transgender people already seek help for because we suffer from having a body that does not match our mind. In addition, we deal with our rejection from society, with those who slam us for having this mental health condition in the first place, and those who don't believe it's a real thing.

Leelah's suicide note includes:[22]

If you are reading this, it means that I have committed suicide and obviously failed to delete this post from my queue.

Please don't be sad, it's for the better. The life I would've lived isn't worth living in... because I'm transgender. I could go into detail explaining why I feel that way, but this note is probably going to be lengthy enough as it is. To put it simply, I feel like a girl trapped in a boy's body, and I've felt that way ever since I was 4. I never knew there was a word for that feeling, nor was it possible for a boy to become a girl, so I never told anyone and I just continued to do traditionally "boyish" things to try to fit in.

When I was 14, I learned what transgender meant and cried of happiness. After 10 years of confusion I finally understood who I was. I immediately told my mom, and she reacted extremely negatively, telling me that it was a phase, that I would never truly be a girl, that God doesn't make mistakes, that I am wrong. If you are reading this, parents, please don't tell this to your kids. Even if you are Christian or are against transgender people don't ever say that to someone, especially your kid. That won't do anything but make them hate them self. That's exactly what it did to me. My mom started taking me to a therapist, but would only take me to christian therapists, (who were all very biased) so I never actually got the therapy I needed to cure me of my depression. I only got more christians telling me that I was selfish and wrong and that I should look to God for help.

When I was 16 I realized that my parents would never come around, and that I would have to wait until I was 18 to start any sort of transitioning treatment, which absolutely broke my heart. The longer you wait, the harder it is to transition. I felt hopeless, that I was just going to look like a man in drag for the rest of my life. On my 16th birthday, when I didn't receive consent from my parents to start transitioning, I cried myself to sleep...

So they took me out of public school, took away my laptop and phone, and forbid me of getting on any sort of social media, completely isolating me from my friends. This was probably the part of my life when I was the most depressed, and I'm surprised I didn't kill myself. I was completely alone for 5 months. No friends, no support, no love. Just my parent's disappointment and the cruelty of loneliness.

Zack Ford, in *Study Suggests Anti-Trans Parents May Literally Be Killing Their Kids*, writes:[23]

Rejection from family members seems to have a significant influence on the health of transgender people, a new study finds. Trans people whose spouses, parents, or children chose not to speak with them after transitioning experienced much higher rates of suicide attempts and substance abuse.

The study, conducted by researchers at the City University of New York, used data from the 2011 National Transgender Discrimination Survey (NTDS), which found that 41 percent of respondents had attempted suicide, far above the national average—1.6 percent of the general population. According to the new analysis, how trans people have been treated by their family was a significant factor for that outcome.

He concludes:

Sarit Golub, one of the researchers on the study, explained to Reuters Health, "For transgender or gender non-conforming individuals, this rejection is based on a failure to accept a fundamental part of that individual's identity—what they feel to be their core self. We are saddened by these findings, and believe they are a call to action for those who work with and care about the transgender community."

The results also further rebut the myth that transitioning itself contributes to transgender people's negative health outcomes. Indeed, the research suggests that family acceptance may actually have a protective effect against these outcomes.

It is horrifying to me to learn that anti-trans activists would rather drive their children to suicide than to allow them to be happily transitioned. That is child abuse of the lowest form.

Transgender-Affirming Therapies and Persistence

Reading *When Harry Became Sally* might lead people into thinking that trans activists are rushing children into sex changes and that the children end up regretting it. Reality check: That is just not what is happening.

In *CALM DOWN: It's Absurd to Claim That Trans Kids Are Being 'Rushed' Into Transitioning: Ignore the alarmist commentators. Parents of trans kids are not rushing their offspring through transitioning. The process is sensitively and carefully overseen*, Samantha Allen writes:[24]

> With headlines like "Why Transgender Kids Should Wait to Transition" and "Push for Children to Choose Gender Identities Early Could Backfire," these articles paint a picture of a world in which children are being rushed through transition at a young age.
> But if you ignore the often-superficial media controversy around this issue—and talk to experts who are actually working with the families of transgender and gender non-conforming children—a more boring truth begins to emerge: Helping children transition is nowhere near as ill-advised and irreversible as you may have been warned. In fact, it can be life-saving.

In the article, Kristina Olson, an associate professor of psychology at the University of Washington and director of the TransYouth Project at UW's Social Cognitive Development Lab, explained that while some families allow freedom of gender expression without social transition, "They aren't just a boy who likes dresses—they feel that they are, in fact, a girl." The article continues:

> "There appears to be no harm—and possible benefit—from such parent-supported early social transitions."

She explains the WPATH requirements and methods. It takes time and certain ages and stages are required before moving on to next steps. She continues:

> That leaves plenty of time along the way for children, families, and mental health professionals to make decisions together—especially at the early and fully reversible stage of social transition.

Lily Durwood, a UW graduate student and co-author of Olson's study, added, "The characterization that families are making this decision flippantly, or that it happens with no thought process going into it, isn't the story we hear from families who have already made the decision."

They criticized the recent media hand-wringing over social transition for transgender kids, which is often fueled by speculation and personal anecdotes. It is worth noting that in *When Harry Became Sally*, all of the frightening stories were carefully selected anecdotes featuring detransition and no success stories, of which are the vast majority. The article continues:

> There are many children, Malpas says, who seem happy to adopt an expansive gender expression without socially transitioning—and it's no surprise that some of these children would grow up to change that expression later in life. But there are also children who are "consistent, persistent, and insistent" that they are, in fact, another gender. And that's when transition seems to help.

"It is only when a child has been very clear for a long period of time in a way that's consistent in different contexts with their parents, with other people in their families, and with providers when they're working with professionals that we then support the family in making that decision of doing a social transition."

Davis said he understands that outside observers with limited experience in the field might be concerned that clinicians are "shuttling [children] through transition very quickly."

"In reality, that's not at all what's happening," he stated definitively.

They further discuss what fuels the desistence myth—lumping non-trans kids with children with actual gender dysphoria. Most of those kids do not need transitioning. But some do. They continue:

> To deny or delay transition—and later, medical treatment—to "consistent, persistent, and insistent" transgender children simply because there is a larger population of children who are gender non-conforming is, Tannehill argued, to throw the baby out with the bathwater.
>
> And trying to convince transgender children that they're not *really* transgender—as medical associations have been clear—is unethical.

A main takeaway from the article is this: there are children who are "consistent, persistent, and insistent" that they are, in fact, another gender. And that's when transition seems to help.

Proper diagnosis, as already discussed, is key. If the child is gender variant, let them be. They may indeed grow up to be cisgender. Punishing them for just happening to be tomboyish might not be the best idea. That is just who they are.

A small percentage of children really are transgender, through no fault of their own and through no fault of the parents. As we have seen, people are born this way. It may be due to genetics or chemicals (endocrine disruptors or drugs such as DES) or other mechanisms. The bottom line is that for many, gender identity is binary, and if it conflicts with their assigned sex, it can cause great distress if left untreated, or, especially, the child is abused because of it.

A responsible therapist will help such a child rather than punish them for it.

When a child is assessed, and a distinction made between gender variant and transgender, a caring parent may opt to help their child socially transition to their inborn gender role. Such a step is always reversible.

Does this help the child? Often, it does. If not, they can always socially transition back. Kristina R. Olson et al. examined the outcomes of social transition of 73 transgender prepubescent children along with control groups of nontransgender children in the same age range. They found:[25]

> Socially transitioned transgender children who are supported in their gender identity have developmentally normative levels of depression and only minimal elevations in anxiety, suggesting that psychopathology is not inevitable within this group. Especially striking is the comparison with reports of children with GID; socially transitioned transgender children have notably lower rates of internalizing psychopathology than previously reported among children with GID living as their natal sex.

That is to say that social transition was indeed helpful. They fared better than those denied social transition.

If the child continues to thrive and are happier in their desired (or insisted) gender role, and do not desist, puberty suppressing drugs may be the next step if that is deemed proper by all parties involved. This will help them avoid the "wrong" puberty and the unwanted secondary sex characteristics which can be expensive to partially ameliorate. The "wrong" puberty can also lead to being outed as trans, in turn leading to discrimination, violence, or worse.

A. L deVries et al., in their report, *Puberty suppression in adolescents with gender identity disorder: a prospective follow-up study*,[26] examined 70 children who were transgendered and were treated with puberty-suppressing medication. None dropped out of the therapy (a zero percent desistance rate) and all continued to the next step—cross-sex hormone treatment. They concluded, "Puberty suppression may be considered a valuable contribution in the clinical management of gender dysphoria in adolescents."

Another study[27] in San Diego of 42 such patients also showed a zero percent desistance rate.

Surgical therapy ("sex change surgeries") are not performed on children or adolescents. If this step is deemed optimal, it is discussed with the patient as a legal adult. The patient may opt not to undergo this step.

"Locking Out" Transgender Identities

When Harry Became Sally, like many anti-trans activists, scaremongers lay people by claiming that most transgender children actually have fluid genders and will naturally turn cisgender, and thus all gender-variant children (actual trans kids included) should be denied transition, else a non-trans child might end up transitioning, and they would end up a statistic to brag about.

There are many things wrong with this. First, the separation of gender-variant and trans kids should be made. Gender-variant children should be allowed to be themselves without stigmatizing them. Trans kids, once properly diagnosed, can socially transition if they wish and it makes them happy. They can always transition back. Hormones and surgery are not given to children, so calm down.

Second, the ideology that all children should be denied treatment, because a non-trans child could (just might!) end up transitioning, while allowing actual transgender children to suffer by being denied treatment (because trans children are, well, trans; who cares if they suffer; chalk up another statistic!) shows utter contempt for them.

Transitioning can be lifesaving. But since they are trans, their lives do not matter to our anti-trans activists. There is a double standard.

Julia Serano makes some good points in her lengthy *Detransition, Desistance, and Disinformation: A Guide for Understanding Transgender Children Debates*.[28] We read:

> As discussed in step #6, the theme of these pieces is that something must be done to stop these cisgender-kids-being-turned-transgender, and the implicit solution is to curtail/limit/end childhood gender transition. Yet, in these pieces there is absolutely no consideration of how this might impact trans children who might benefit from gender transition. In fact, such oversights can lead to obvious hypocrisy. For example, authors often raise fears that some children (i.e., ones who are "really cisgender" in their minds) may be pushed into the "wrong" puberty, and thus may have to undergo expensive medical procedures to correct those bodily changes. But this precisely describes what a trans child would face if they were not allowed to transition until adulthood. *If the former example concerns you, but the latter one doesn't, then that's a clear sign that you value cis bodies and lives over trans ones.* (her emphasis)

Along similar lines, these articles invariably raise fears about children being placed on puberty blockers and hormones, and question whether someone so young can make such an important and potentially irreversible decision about their own body. But consider a cisgender girl who has always been happy with her assigned gender. Then suddenly, at the age of nine or ten (as she is entering puberty), her body shows signs of masculinization, and doctors confirm that this is due to her body producing testosterone (for the record, this is not a hypothetical situation for some intersex children). If this child was horrified about these potential unwanted changes, and asked for hormonal intervention (which the doctor confirmed would be safe and effective), would you respect her decision and allow her to proceed with it? Or would you dismiss her wishes on account of her lack of maturity, and insist that she just deal with the testosterone until she is eighteen and capable of making an adult decision? As with the last example, if this scenario concerns you, but the idea of transgender children being forced to experience unwanted puberties does not, then you clearly value cis bodies and lives over trans ones.

Let's not attack good medicine

The WPATH Standards of Care (SoC) are designed to provide the best care for the patient. This includes children and adolescents. The SoC are to help treat both gender nonconforming and transgender people. The diagnosis is done via the most up-to-date DSM, which requires children to be insistent in order to be diagnosed with gender dysphoria and treated as such. Gender nonconforming children can be treated in other ways.

For treatment of gender dysphoria, we read in the WPATH SoC, those who treat children must be competent:

The following are recommended minimum credentials for mental health professionals who assess, refer, and offer therapy to children and adolescents presenting with gender dysphoria:

1. Meet the competency requirements for mental health professionals working with adults, as outlined in section VII;

2. Trained in childhood and adolescent developmental psychopathology;

3. Competent in diagnosing and treating the ordinary problems of children and adolescents.

There are guidelines in assessment:

When assessing children and adolescents who present with gender dysphoria, mental health professionals should broadly conform to the following guidelines:

1. Mental health professionals should not dismiss or express a negative attitude towards nonconforming gender identities or indications of gender dysphoria. Rather, they should acknowledge the presenting concerns of children, adolescents, and their families; offer a thorough assessment for gender dysphoria and any co-existing mental health concerns; and educate clients and their families about therapeutic options, if needed. Acceptance and removal of secrecy can bring considerable relief to gender dysphoric children/adolescents and their families.

2. Assessment of gender dysphoria and mental health should explore the nature and characteristics of a child's or adolescent's gender identity. A psychodiagnostic and psychiatric assessment – covering the areas of emotional functioning, peer and other social relationships, and intellectual functioning/school achievement – should be performed. Assessment should include an evaluation of the strengths and weaknesses of family functioning. Emotional and behavioral problems are relatively common, and unresolved issues in a child's or youth's environment may be present (de Vries, Doreleijers, Steensma, & Cohen-

Kettenis, 2011; Di Ceglie & Thümmel, 2006; Wallien et al., 2007).

3. For adolescents, the assessment phase should also be used to inform youth and their families about the possibilities and limitations of different treatments. This is necessary for informed consent, but also important for assessment. The way that adolescents respond to information about the reality of sex reassignment can be diagnostically informative. Correct information may alter a youth's desire for certain treatment, if the desire was based on unrealistic expectations of its possibilities.

Social transition is up to the parents (not the professional or the child). One option is for the child to act in the role of their identified gender part time, for instance. It is also stressed that a social transition does not need to be permanent. The SoC continues:

Mental health professionals can help families to make decisions regarding the timing and process of any gender role changes for their young children. They should provide information and help parents to weigh the potential benefits and challenges of particular choices. Relevant in this respect are the previously described relatively low persistence rates of childhood gender dysphoria (Drummond et al., 2008; Wallien & Cohen-Kettenis, 2008). A change back to the original gender role can be highly distressing and even result in postponement of this second social transition on the child's part (Steensma & Cohen-Kettenis, 2011). For reasons such as these, parents may want to present this role change as an exploration of living in another gender role, rather than an irreversible situation. Mental health professionals can assist parents in identifying potential in between solutions or compromises (e.g., only when on vacation). It is also important that parents explicitly let the child know that there is a way back.

Regardless of a family's decisions regarding transition (timing, extent), professionals should counsel and support them as they work through the options and implications. If parents do not allow their young child to make a gender role transition, they may need counseling to assist them with meeting their child's needs in a sensitive and nurturing way, ensuring that the child has ample possibilities to explore gender feelings and behavior in a safe environment. If parents do allow their young child to make a gender role transition, they may need counseling to facilitate a positive experience for their child. For example, they may need support in using correct pronouns, maintaining a safe and supportive environment for their transitioning child (e.g., in school, peer group settings), and communicating with other people in their child's life. In either case, as a child nears puberty, further assessment may be needed as options for physical interventions become relevant.

The SoC were written with the best interest if the child in mind. But parents have the final say. For those that do transition, we have already read that they fare just as well as their cisgender counterparts.

Children need our protection and guidance. We need medical professionals who will help them mature in harmony with the identities, rather than deploy debunked, harmful, nonscientific conversion/reparative therapies aimed at changing their brain structures. And we need a culture that cultivates a sound understanding of inborn gender identity and how it is rooted in the biology of the brain.

CHAPTER SEVEN

Gender and Nonconformance

I am not quite sure what Ryan T. Anderson's point was with his *Gender and Culture* chapter, other than perhaps to say that men and women are different, and never the twain shall they meet. It seems to be stressing a belief that transgender people should not be allowed to transition, as well as that gays should not be allowed to marry or have children.

I'm game. Let us go with a gender discussion.

The impressionist painter, Auguste Renoir (1841-1919), often painted people, especially women, in daily activities. He also painted his children. Here are two of them:

It looks like we have one girl sewing on the left and another playing with toy soldiers on the right. One of these looks gender-atypical, yes? We think that a girl sewing is gender appropriate activity but not playing with toy soldiers—that is a boy activity. We have gender conforming behavior on the left and gender nonconforming behavior on the right.

But, using my Laurence Fishburne Morpheus voice, what if I told you...

Both kids are boys.

We have Jean Renior (1894-1979) on the left and Claude "Coco" Renior (1901-1969) on the right. So, our gender-atypical behavior seems to have suddenly switched. We now have gender nonconforming behavior on the left (a boy sewing) and gender conforming behavior on the right (a boy playing with toy soldiers).

I would argue, though, that it should be fine for boys to sew and for girls to play with toy soldiers.

More than that, those boys do look like girls at first glance, yes? Was dressing the boys up like that and giving them long hair with ribbons damaging? Hardly. This was a typical way that boys dressed at the time. Look at my [slightly distant] cousin, Franklin Delano Roosevelt, in his spiffy getup. That did not affect him negatively—he grew up to defend the world against fascism.

Gender roles can change through time. Pink is for girls and blue is for boys, right? Not always. In a June 1918 article from the trade publication *Earnshaw's Infants' Department* said, "The generally accepted rule is pink for the boys, and blue for the girls. The reason is that pink, being a more decided and stronger color, is more suitable for the boy, while blue, which is more delicate and dainty, is prettier for the girl."[1]

In 1927, *Time* magazine printed a chart showing sex-appropriate colors for girls and boys according to leading U.S. stores. In Boston, Filene's told parents to dress boys in pink. So did Best & Co. in New York City, Halle's in Cleveland and Marshall Field in Chicago.[2]

But since he brought it up, we see that on page 167 of *When Harry Became Sally*, Ryan T. Anderson writes:

> The best sociological evidence available, controlling for other factors including poverty and even genetics, indicates that both boys and girls fare best on virtually every indicator examined...when they are raised by their wedded biological parents.

That sounds like an opinion, but perhaps two parents are better than one and that kids do well when raised by their own parents (but sometimes one parent dies or otherwise separate; should the kids be taken away from the single parent, Dr. Anderson?). However, he links that opinion to an endnote. And in it, he discusses not only his own anti-gay book, *Truth Overruled*, in which he argues against same-sex parenting, but he also points us to an article by the Witherspoon Institute.

The Witherspoon Institute! This is the same extreme right-wing propaganda organization[3] that paid Mark Regnerus, a University of Texas professor, $700,000[4] to write a report claiming that children with same-sex parents were worse off than children of straight parents.

He did not really compare straight parents to gay parents. Rather, he effectively compared families with two always-married straight parents to some families who only had one parent but were characterized as households headed by gay fathers or lesbian mothers.[5] That is, he compared straight parents to broken homes, and claimed that the broken homes were single gay parents. He did not study two-parent gay parents at all.

He did not even ask if the single parents were gay. "I didn't ask them whether they thought their mom was a lesbian or if their dad was gay," Regnerus said. "Because, in part, self-identity is a different kind of thing than behavior, and lot of people weren't 'out' in that era." Yep. Just examine a single parent and label them as gay.

His sham "study" is described as:[6]

> Mark Regnerus' flawed paper in the journal Social Science Research claiming that gay parenting harms children has been widely criticized by major medical organizations and over 200 professors across the country, while hate groups and ex-gay ministries have defended it. There are many indications that the paper was published as a political calculation, and the University of Texas has agreed to investigate whether it constitutes scientific misconduct. Now, a member of the journal's editorial board has completed an internal audit of the study and found it to be "bullshit."

Back to the Witherspoon Institute; the one that handsomely paid professor Regnerus to write his bogus anti-gay propaganda "study". We read, in *Witherspoon Institute reintroduces hate group CanaVox for about the fourth time*:[7]

> Witherspoon Institute is an extreme-orthodox Catholic organization founded by Robert P. George and Luis E. Tellez. Telles is an Opus Dei numerary (a secular celibate). George and Tellez were two of the original incorporaters of National Organization for Marriage and continue to serve on its board of directors.
>
> Witherspoon provides a pretentious pseudo-intellectual blog called Public Discourse. It is edited by Ryan T. Anderson and features a variety of miscreants and crackpots as authors.

Witherspoon organized, designed and provided most of the grant money for Mark Regnerus' thoroughly discredited New Family Structures study. It was intended to demonstrate that gay couples are crappy parents in order to undermine marriage equality. Witherspoon created a website dedicated to the study and proclaimed it as proof that gay couples are crappy parents. This was supposed to influence the Supreme Court as it considered United States v. Windsor in 2013. The proof went poof. It all backfired as people realized that the conclusions regarding same-sex parenting were based on research that did not seem to include same-sex parents. There were other problems as well and it ruined Regnerus' reputation.

So much for making their point about gays making crappy parents. Now, let's look at the facts.

The Dutch study, *A Population-Based Comparison of Female and Male Same-Sex Parent and Different-Sex Parent Households*,[8] of 25,250 families showed that:

> Multivariate analysis of covariance for the structural comparison between female same-sex parent and different same-sex households (mother reports) showed no significant effect for children's psychological well-being, problems in the parent–child relationship, perceived parental competency, and informal and formal support in child-rearing...
>
> For fathers in same- and different-sex parent households, MANCOVA showed no significant household type effect for children's psychological well-being, problems in the parent–child relationship, perceived parental competency, and informal and formal support in child-rearing.

That is, kids in same-sex households fared no different that opposite-sex households. The report by the American Academy of Pediatrics states:[9]

Extensive data available from more than 30 years of research reveal that children raised by gay and lesbian parents have demonstrated resilience with regard to social, psychological, and sexual health despite economic and legal disparities and social stigma. Many studies have demonstrated that children's well-being is affected much more by their relationships with their parents, their parents' sense of competence and security, and the presence of social and economic support for the family than by the gender or the sexual orientation of their parents.

An amicus brief countering the sham Regnerus study states that children of same-sex parents *fared better* than those of opposite-sex parents:[10]

In their briefs to the Court, the Bipartisan Legal Advisory Group of the U.S. House of Representatives ("BLAG"), the Hollingsworth Petitioners (the "Proposition 8 Proponents"), and their respective amici assert that children fare better with opposite-sex parents than with same-sex parents.

On page 167 of *When Harry Became Sally*, Ryan T. Anderson writes:

Even on a biological level, Wilcox adds, a father's presence affects his daughter, as the pheromones released from his body slow down her sexual development. That makes her less likely to experience early puberty...

Dad's funky smell is a puberty-suppressing drug? I thought that Dr. Anderson was against that sort of thing.

Gender-appropriate behavior and clothing can vary over cultures and with time. In Western cultures, it was common for a grown man to wear, essentially, a knee-length dress, tights, and Mary Jane shoes in the medieval era, such an outfit is generally reserved for girls now.

124

Behavior is something else. Boys have generally been expected to be rough and girls meek. But that does not always happen. Some kids who are not transgendered nonetheless have behavior that is not deemed "gender appropriate." Tomboys do exist. As we have read, rather than accepting that Jamison spoke and acted more like a boy, speech therapy was done and surgery was considered to feminize his voice. I would argue that people should have just let him be.

Three years of conversion therapy in mental institutions and a million dollars did not turn Daphne Scholinski girly.

When evaluating gender-variant children, deciding on the optimal treatment should be based on each individual child. All are different. Some really are transgendered. The DSM-5 criteria are now fairly strict. A transgendered child is likely one that is insistent and persistent. Eventual transition and medical interventions may be best for them. But many (or most) gender-variant children are not transgendered. Nor are they to be counted as desisters. They are just gender variant. For them, affirmation rather than conversion therapy are likely optimal.

If a girl is a Tomboy, so what? She is not hurting anyone. She may have been exposed to more prenatal androgens than other girls or there may be other reasons why she is not naturally as girly as others.

A boy might want to wear a dress, yet not want to be or insist that they are a girl. It seems OK to let them wear one.

I recall the 2000 Shirley MacLaine movie, *The Dress Code* (a.k.a. *Bruno*).[11] In it, a boy named Bruno likes to wear dresses. He is also an expert speller, and likes to wear dresses at spelling bees. But, he goes to a Catholic school, and they make his life difficult at first.

He does not relent, and continues in the spelling bee contests wearing dresses ("they're holy vestments," he insists). Sometimes, women and girls would cheer him on in the audience while wearing the same outfits as Bruno. If he can with nationals, he will be rewarded with a visit with the Pope (whom he points out, also wears a dress).

It is a story of acceptance of a child who is different.

And that makes me think of the warming 2012 novel by R. J. Palacio, *Wonder*.[12] It is about the difficulties experiences by a 10-year-old boy with a craniofacial condition (his face looks very unusual) and that makes socializing difficult and prone to ostracism. But it is also a journey for those in his school and neighborhood towards acceptance. It wasn't his fault that he was born like that.

Nor is it the fault of a gender-variant child or a transgendered child. I would argue for acceptance.

The anti-trans activists insist that, for transgender people, rejection of their inborn identities is best. Seriously, that is just cruel.

Dr. Anderson seems to be telling us that the idea of trans or gender variant acceptance (affirmation) is brand new; just a few months old. And that it is scary and dangerous and that planes will fall out of the sky if we affirm someone's inborn identity if the identity is not cisgendered

It won't. Nor is it a new idea.

Marlo Thomas wanted to teach her young niece that she could be whatever she wanted, but had difficulty in finding books without gender stereotyping. She relates:[13]

> I told my sister Terre "it would take Dionne 30 years to get over it (traditional stories) the same as it took all of us. We need to find her some different books to read" and she said "You go and find 'em". Well there weren't any. And not only that, I was in the bookstore one day looking around and found this one (picture book) that showed a pilot on one page and a stewardess on a facing page (with a caption) that said "Boys are pilots, girls are stewardesses." Well I nearly had a heart attack right there in the bookstore, so I said "We'll make a record for Dionne".

So, she brought a number of musicians together to make an album named *Free to Be... You and Me*. That was in 1972. The basic concept was to encourage post-1960s gender neutrality, saluting values such as individuality, tolerance, and comfort with one's identity. A major thematic message is that anyone—whether a boy or a girl—can achieve anything.[14]

Among the artists who participated were Michael Jackson, Shirley Jones, Diana Ross, and Rosey Greer. Rosey Greer is a football legend who was guarding Ethel Kennedy, during the Robert F. Kennedy assassination. Although unable to prevent that killing, Grier took control of the gun and subdued the shooter, Sirhan Sirhan.[15] Yet he sang, on the album, *It's All Right to Cry*. He also enjoys needlepoint and macramé.[16]

Now, nearly 50 years after Marlo Thomas's gender equality album, I still agree. Let people be free to be who they are. This includes gender-variant children as well as transgendered children.

Feel free to stick to rigid gender stereotypes yourself if you wish, but do not stigmatize those that are naturally different.

Culture Club Cultivates

Our anti-trans moment arose in part from a rebellion against the innate differences within each gender. These innate differences from rigid stereotypes are often stigmatized. But they are natural. Depending on prenatal hormones, genetics, or other causes, some girls are more masculine than average and some boys are less.

Actually, I am not at all sure where Anderson was going with his "Cultures Cultivate" section, so I will go along for the ride.

But in that manner, did it really bother anyone that Boy George of Culture Club band was considered to look like a girl? How about 1970s bands? Young dudes in rock bands in that time often looked like girls to me. For that matter, High School boys did, too. Long hair was in, as were frilly blouses on guys (think of Robert Plant, the members of Yes, and other popular bands of the 1970s).

As mentioned in the first paragraph of this section, individual boys and girls may naturally vary from stereotypical behavior. Gender identity and expression are not binary. For that matter, neither are physical sexes. Some men and some women will have more, or less, body and facial hair than other men and women. Body shapes differ. Some men and women naturally have Adam's apples and some do not. Karyotypes differ. Genitalia differs. So too is attraction. We know that some people are heterosexual; some are homosexual; some are bisexual; some are asexual. And there are degrees of that as well.

Sexual orientation falls on a spectrum. Sex falls on a spectrum (male, female, various forms of intersex, and many places in between). And due to prenatal forces, gender identity falls on a spectrum. Many have binary identities, transgender people included; but some people's gender identity does not develop to either male or female in utero, but may be between or neither.

A good graphic for this is the Gender Unicorn, pictured on the next page. It was created by the Trans Students Educational Resources (TSER).[17]

The Gender Unicorn

🧠 Gender Identity
- Female/Woman/Girl
- Male/Man/Boy
- Other Gender(s)

Gender Expression
- Feminine
- Masculine
- Other

Sex Assigned at Birth
Female   Male   Other/Intersex

💗 Physically Attracted to
- Women
- Men
- Other Gender(s)

❤️ Emotionally Attracted to
- Women
- Men
- Other Gender(s)

To learn more, go to:
www.transstudent.org/gender

Design by Landyn Pan and Anna Moore

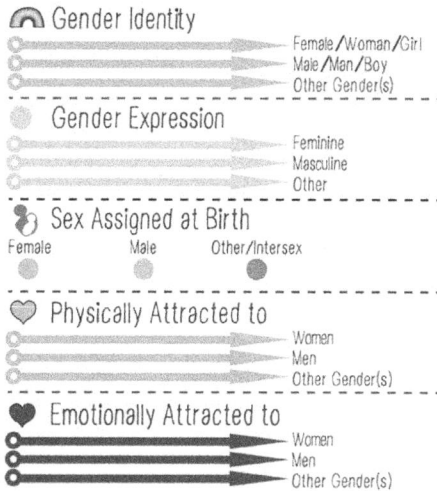

The Gender Unicorn: gender, sex, orientation, etc. lie on a spectrum.

Since gender identity and expression vary, then the best therapy for the parents may be to let them be. If a parent is worried that their child may be transgendered, it may be best to ask the child what they are. Their response may be the biggest clue as to whether they are trans or gender variant/gender nonconforming.

If they are trans, don't worry. It is not their fault (or yours). They can, as we have seen, live wonderful lives if they are not stigmatized or punished with conversion therapy. Social transition might (or might not) be the best thing for them.

If they are gender variant or nonconforming, don't worry. Again, it is not their fault. Forcing them into a rigid stereotype might result in poor well-being and resentment. Allowing them to thrive may indeed be best thing for the child. For instance, if a boy likes wearing dresses, and then they are told that only girls can wear dresses, they may want to socially transition into a female role in order to do so, even if they are not transgender.

They then might end up being chalked up as a "desister" and give anti-trans activists reason to celebrate. No. If they were simply allowed to be a boy that is allowed to wear a dress, and they really are not trans, there need not be any transition and will not be incorrectly-labeled as a "desister."

CHAPTER EIGHT

Policies That Don't Suck

On 2 February 2010, Rhiannon O'Donnabhain and other transgender patients breathed a sigh of relief. The US Tax Court ruled for the first time that treatment for gender identity disorder qualifies as medical care under the Internal Revenue Code, and is therefore deductible.[1]

In 2002, Ms. O'Donnabhain filed her return claiming medical expenses, but was then audited. The IRS refused her deduction.

Medical deductions for medically necessary treatment were generally allowed, except for transgender patients.

It took years of fighting, but the IRS finally opted to end its blatantly discriminatory rules against trans people.

Ideology

Gender identity policies are just about letting people be their true selves, and to pee in peace. Anti-transgender ideologies are not just about preserving the right to discriminate against LGB [and especially] T citizens, but, for transgender citizens, to refuse all dignity. The most reprehensible resolution passed so far this year was the Kansas Republican Party's to "oppose all efforts to validate transgender identity."[2] This resolution, which aims to dehumanize a section of the population, is one of the most troubling so far this year.

Equality Kansas responded with:[3]

Yesterday afternoon, the Kansas Republican Party adopted a hateful anti-science, anti-trans policy that demeans and dehumanizes transgender Kansans, particularly transgender children. The author of the resolution, Sam Brownback's son-in-law Eric Teetsel, claimed it was a matter of "dignity."

No.

Denying science and attacking schoolchildren in the name of religion is not a recognition of "dignity." This is a cheap election year attack by Sam Brownback's son-in-law, and yet another attempt to dehumanize those who do not fit inside the narrow world view of Brownback, his family, and his wing of the Republican party. Equality Kansas is incredibly disappointed that Kansas Republicans, on a day they should be focused on protecting children, promote such an undignified and crass assault.

Tom Witt, executive director of Equality Kansas, continues:[4]

"It's disheartening to see Sam Brownback's son-in-law Eric Teetsel cite discredited junk science to justify continued discrimination," Witt said in an email. "Teetsel's recent statement doubles down on bigotry, and contrary to his claims of 'compassion and concern,' displays an utter disregard for the lives of transgender Kansans. If he wants to know why so many transgender people attempt suicide, he and his shrinking circle of allies need look no further than a mirror."

What makes this so insidious can be seen when we examine Genocide Watch's The Ten Stages of Genocide by Dr. Gregory Stanton.[5] Briefly, this is:

1. CLASSIFICATION: All cultures have categories to distinguish people into "us and them".

2. SYMBOLIZATION: We give names or other symbols to the classifications.

3. DISCRIMINATION: A dominant group uses law, custom, and political power to deny the rights of other groups.

4. DEHUMANIZATION: One group denies the humanity of the other group.

5. ORGANIZATION: Genocide is always organized, usually by the state.

6. POLARIZATION: Extremists drive the groups apart. Hate groups broadcast polarizing propaganda.

7. PREPARATION: National or perpetrator group leaders plan the "Final Solution" to the targeted group.

8. PERSECUTION: Victims are identified and separated out.

9. EXTERMINATION begins, and quickly becomes the mass killing legally called "genocide." It is "extermination" to the killers because they do not believe their victims to be fully human.

10. DENIAL is the final stage that lasts throughout and always follows a genocide.

In the USA, several of these are already actively being used. For instance:

Classification: There is the classification of transgender and cisgender.

Symbolization: Transgender people already and proudly have their own flag.[6]

Discrimination: Certainly, transgender discrimination exists, and there are bills in several states aimed at legalizing trans discrimination on the basis of religion.

Dehumanization: The Kansas resolution discussed above is clearly dehumanizing.

Organization: there are many anti-LGBT and anti-T hate groups operating in the USA. The Southern Poverty Law Center lists several of them.[7]

Polarization: Trans rights (and LGBT rights) is a highly polarized issue, with the vast majority of Republicans supporting anti-trans/anti-LGBT legislation and the vast majority of Democrats opposing such bills.

Preparation: As we saw in the introduction, the Family Research Council has laid down a five step program for eradicating transgender people from American life.[8]

Persecution: As The New Republic stated:[9]

Transgender people are some of the least protected, most persecuted people in the United States. In a recent study of transgender students, nearly half said they'd been "punched, kicked, or injured with a weapon" at least once in the last year. On average, a transgender person is murdered because of their identity every month, according to the Transgender Legal Defense and Education Fund. In 2008, for instance, Angie Zapata, an 18-year-old Colorado woman, was bludgeoned to death with a fire extinguisher when her attacker—a man she met through a social-networking site—realized that she was born male.

They also described the following:

On April 18, a transgender woman named Chrissy Lee Polis went to the women's bathroom in a Baltimore County McDonald's. When she came out, two teenage girls approached and spat in her face. Then they threw her to the floor and started kicking her in the head. As a crowd of customers watched, Polis tried to stand up, but the girls dragged her by her hair across the restaurant, ripping the carrings out of her ears. The last thing Polis remembers, before she had a seizure, was spitting blood on the restaurant door. The incident made national news—not because this sort of violence against transgender people is unusual, but because a McDonald's employee recorded the beating on his cell phone and posted the video on YouTube.

It is not uncommon for a transgender person to be murdered. Wikipedia[10] lists 11 trans murder in the USA in 2014, 23 in 2015, 28 in 2016, and another 28 in 2017.

Yet, right-leaning politicians continue to write anti-transgender bills and refuse to endorse anti-discrimination bills. And these are bills that are in no way configured to do anyone any good. Their purposes include spite and to set people against the transgender population.

What laws would make sense to everyone involved? We will now discuss them.

Privacy

As stated in the Media Matters article *A Comprehensive Guide To The Debunked "Bathroom Predator" Myth*:[11]

> Conservatives have long peddled the myth that sexual predators will exploit nondiscrimination laws to sneak into women's restrooms by pretending to be transgender. The "bathroom predator" myth has been repeatedly debunked—by experts and government officials in 16 states and the District of Columbia, and school administrators in 23 school districts and four universities. Despite overwhelming evidence, many media outlets continue to uncritically repeat the debunked myth peddled by anti-LGBT groups.

Should transgender be banned from public facilities out of a remote fear that they *might* solicit a sex act in a bathroom, just to be safe? Then how about banning

Republican lawmakers? Indeed, More Republican legislators have been arrested for bathroom misconduct than trans people.[12] Does it still make sense?

In schools

Gender variant students already have a difficult time in environments that are not affirming. The Advocate has this cartoon:[13]

In a March 2017 post for The Heritage Foundation and on page 201 of *When Harry Became Sally*, Dr. Anderson posted the following logic map:[14]

Access to Lockers and Showers Under Obama Administration

Access to Girls' Lockers and Showers				Access to Boys' Lockers and Showers		
Sex	Gender Identity	Result		Sex	Gender Identity	Result
Female	Female	Allowed		Male	Male	Allowed
Female	Male	Allowed		Male	Female	Allowed
Male	Female	Allowed		Female	Male	Allowed
Male	Male	Denied		Female	Female	Denied

This is rather silly and not at all very likely applied.

Let me correct the chart:

Access to Girls' Facilities		Access to Boys' Facilities	
Registered at School As	Access	Registered at School As	Access
Male	No	Male	Yes
Female	Yes	Female	No

This is the way that it has been done. I know of many transgender children who have transitioned and those are the rules used.

However, with the laws that Republicans are in the process of passing. The new paradigm will be:

Access to Girls' Facilities				Access to Boys' Facilities		
Sex	Gender Identity	Result		Sex	Gender Identity	Result
Female	Boy	Yelled at		Female	Boy	Banned
Female	Girl	Allowed		Female	Girl	Banned
Male	Boy	Banned		Male	Boy	Allowed
Male	Girl	Banned		Male	Girl	Beaten

This could effectively ban transgender kids from the facilities completely, with the possible exception of single-occupancy rooms (meaning segregation; remember Jim Crow laws?). If a transgendered student uses the facilities allowed, they may be yelled at or beaten. That does not seem like "reasonable accommodation" to me. I propose that students should use the one where they use the facilities for the gender that they are registered as.

Public facilities

Laws that are being proposed in the anti-transgender moment aim to ostracize and harm the transgender population. In the old days, people legally used restrooms according to the following logic:

Allowed in Women's Room		Allowed in Men's Room	
Legally:	Allowed	Legally:	Allowed
Male	No	Male	Yes
Female	Yes	Female	No

But many laws being promoted base sex on that assigned at birth, meaning transmen with a penis would be banned from the men's room (but allowed in the women's?!), and transwomen who have vaginas would be banned from the women's (but allowed in the men's?!). We already saw how ridiculous that is. But that is what anti-transgender activists are pushing.

On the *National Conference of State Legislatures'* website, in their "Bathroom Bill" Legislative Tracking page, posts several bills that restrict public use of facilities to one sex, and many state that sex assigned at birth is the requirement,[15] including the following, as quoted on the site:

> **Arkasas:** *Defines sex as determined by anatomy and genetics existing at the time of birth.*
> **Illinois:** *Defines sex as the physical condition of being male or female, determined by chromosomes and assigned at birth.*

Kansas: *Defines sex as the physical condition of being male or female, determined by chromosomes and assigned at birth.*

Kentucky: *Defines biological sex as the physical condition of being male or female, as determined by chromosomes and assigned at birth.*

Minnesota: *Defines sex as being determined by chromosomes and sex assigned at birth.*

Missouri: *Defines biological sex as the physical condition of being male or female, as determined by a person's chromosomes, assigned at birth.*

Montana: *Defines biological sex as the physical condition of being male or female as assigned at birth.*

New York: *Defines biological sex as the physical condition of being male or female as assigned at birth.*

South Dakota: *Defined biological sex as being determined by anatomy and genetics at the time of birth.*

Tennessee: *sex, as indicated on their original birth certificate.*

Texas: *Defines biological sex as the physical condition of being male or female as assigned at birth.*

Wyoming: *the person's sex assigned at birth.*

If such bills pass, then that will put men in women's rooms and vice versa (or simply not allow a transgender person to use any facility at all; yet we see that if they do, it would, by law, be the *wrong* one).

Anti-trans activists claim that if transgender people (legally living as those of their gender identity) are allowed to use public restrooms, then male predators will dress like women in order to attack women. Nonsense. That is already illegal. And I seriously doubt that a predator will convince a therapist to write a letter for a gender change, then apply for a legal name change. Name changes often require such to be printed in newspapers for a period of time before being granted. Imagine the workplace conversation.

"Hey, Barry; I read that you are changing your name to Mary. What's that about?"

After the legal name change and the letter from a therapist stating that he has gender dysphoria (fat chance of that happening), the perp can get a license with the new name and gender marker. All so that he can legally enter a restroom in order to molest women.

Seriously? This is the fear that activists have? Molesting women in restrooms is already illegal. A perv would not need to go through all that. He would just go and commit the crime. Allowing transgender people to use public facilities will not change that.

For transgendered people, these are the new choices:[16]

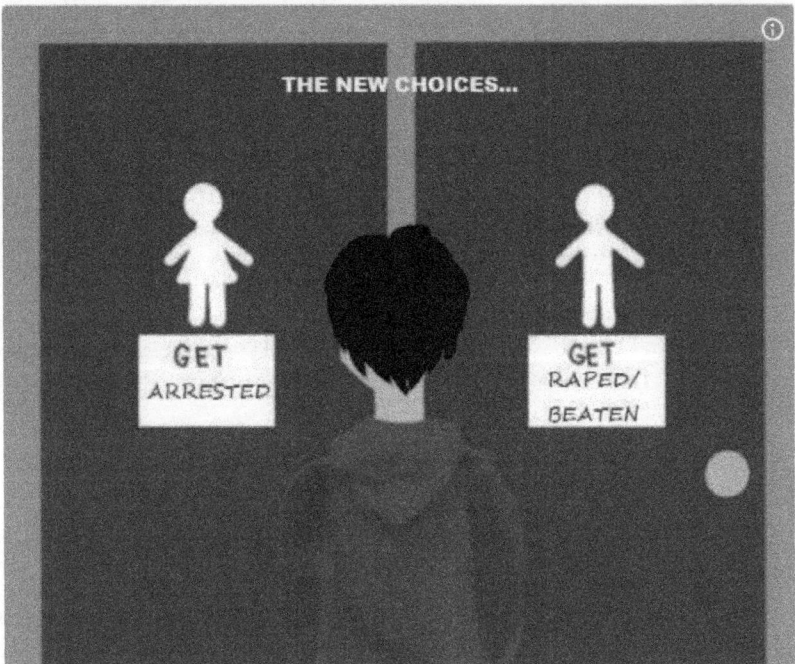

How Would a Cisgender Person be Harmed by a Transgender Person Using a Gender-Appropriate Restroom?

Perhaps The Matrix's Morpheus has the answer:[17]

WHAT IF I TOLD YOU

THAT YOU'VE ALREADY SHARED A BATHROOM WITH A TRANS PERSON AND YOU'RE JUST FINE. YOU DID'T EVEN NOTICE.

Enforcing Discrimination Laws through Orthodoxy

Policies that allow discrimination on the basis of gender identity often do so on the basis of religious freedom. But should one's religious beliefs, even if seriously held, trump the rights of their victims? Must the victims, here, meaning LGBT individuals, lose their rights?

In Stephanie Russell-Kraft's review of Nelson Tebbe's book, *Religious Freedom in an Egalitarian Age,* we read:[18]

It's easy, in the current American political climate, to see religious freedom and LGBT rights as two opposing values, permanently in conflict with each other. Much of this has to do with the backlash to advancements in LGBT rights from conservative religious groups. When the Supreme Court in 2015 affirmed the legal right of same-sex couples to marry, religious freedom laws began making their way through state legislatures and courthouses, demanding exceptions to anti-LGBT discrimination laws for individuals with religiously based views...

The core of the current battle comes down to this: As LGBT individuals have made civil rights gains, religious traditionalists who adhere to certain ideas of gender and sexuality have asked for exemption from non-discrimination laws in health care, housing, employment, adoption, and marriage-related services.

Part of what makes these conflicts seem intractable is the fact that the Constitution does have competing values; the requirements of the free exercise and the establishment clauses, freedom of association, and anti-discrimination on the basis of faith don't always add up. Conservative Christians are increasingly positioning themselves as a threatened minority group in need of special rights: If LGBT persons are granted special legal protection, they argue, so should religious traditionalists. Of course, civil rights laws do not single out religious traditionalists for disparate treatment, but the conflict, however justified, is real.

Of course, LGBT citizens do not want "special rights," they want equal rights. What we have is the conflict between the ability to discriminate against a group of citizens (claiming religious reasons for discrimination) vs. the right of such citizens not to be discriminated against. The recent spate of state "Religious Freedom Restoration Acts" (RFRAs) are clearly aimed at allowing some groups to discriminate against others, in particular, LGBT citizens.

But is it necessary for religions to discriminate against LGBT people? It was once heresy to suggest that the earth revolved around the sun. Galileo was severely punished for suggesting it. But now, this fact is rarely denied, even in churches. We hope that one day, being kind to transgender people (or other groups) will no longer be considered heresy.

In How to Think About Sexual Orientation and Gender Identity (SOGI) Policies and Religious Freedom, Ryan T. Anderson writes:[19]

> "Fairness for All," like other SOGI laws, uses the government and the power of the law to send the message that traditional Judeo–Christian beliefs are not only false, but also discriminatory and rooted in animus.

Some churches clearly are discriminatory and use their religion for animus. But not all Judeo-Christian churches or individuals have such animosity towards LGBT people. In New England, it is actually a common sight to see a rainbow flag flying on a church. They fly it to show that all people are accepted. Many Christians that I know have no animosity towards LGBT people. They call transgender people by their desired names and pronouns, and would not hesitate to assist in a friend's or loved one's same sex marriage.

And I know Christian doctors who do not agree with refusing health care for transgender patients.

Many denominations of several religions not only do not hate LGBT people, but are affirming.[20]

For instance, the Affirming Pentecostal Church International states:[21]

> APCI was born out of a desire to have an organization where those of like precious faith, could accomplish the work of the Kingdom of God as one body.
>
> A body that did not discriminate based on one's Race, Age, Sexual Orientation, Economic Status, Gender, or Background.

The Alliance of Baptists state:[22]

> As Christians and as Baptists, we particularly lament the denigration of our gay, lesbian, bisexual, and transgender sisters and brothers in this debate by those who claim to speak for God. We affirm that the Alliance of Baptists supports the rights of all citizens to full marriage equality, and we affirm anew that the Alliance will "create places of refuge and renewal for those who are ignored by the church."

The Church of England Education Office states:[23]

> This updated version of *Valuing all God's Children* seeks to offer further guidance and support, and places it within this vision. All bullying, including homophobic, biphobic and transphobic bullying causes profound damage, leading to higher levels of mental health disorders, self-harm, depression and suicide.
>
> Central to Christian theology is the truth that every single one of us is made in the image of God. Every one of us is loved unconditionally by God. We must avoid, at all costs, diminishing the dignity of any individual to a stereotype or a problem. Church of England schools offer a community where everyone is a person known and loved by God, supported to know their intrinsic value.
>
> This guidance helps schools to offer the Christian message of love, joy and the celebration of our humanity without exception or exclusion.

The Unitarian Universalist Church states:[24]

> Each of us has worth and dignity, and that worth includes our gender and our sexuality. As Unitarian Universalists (UUs), we not only open our doors to people of all sexual orientations and gender identities, we value diversity of sexuality and gender and see it as a spiritual gift. We create

144

inclusive religious communities and work for LGBTQ justice and equity as a core part of who we are. *All* of who you are is sacred. *All* of who you are is welcome.

In short, one can be a good Christian and not hate LGBT people, or discriminate against them. What would Jesus do? Would He persecute LGBT people? Not the one that I know.

In *Fortune*, Steve Sanders (an associate professor of law at the Indiana University Maurer School of Law) wrote, in *Commentary: 'Religious Liberty' Is Not an Excuse to Deny Transgender People Medical Care*:[25]

> The Trump administration is developing a policy that would empower health care workers to refuse to participate in abortions or treat transgender patients. According to *Politico*, the new rules would punish health care organizations that don't give employees an opportunity to object to treating patients for religious or moral reasons. The Department of Health and Human Services is creating a new division within its Office of Civil Rights to investigate such complaints.
>
> This is a perilous new policy, as it has the potential to impede access to care, insult the dignity of patients, and allow religious beliefs to override mainstream medical science...
>
> Caution also is necessary with accommodations because often there is no way to differentiate between genuine religious convictions and beliefs that are made up out of convenience. Because religious beliefs are inherently personal and not subject to conventional forms of proof, an employer is usually powerless to question them. And so an employee who merely has a phobia toward transgender people might still claim a "religious" exemption, and the employer would have little choice but to grant it.

He has a very good point. One would be able to deny a service, such as medicine, to a transgender person, who insists that they have had lifelong gender dysphoria and are suffering from it, by denying that transgender identities even exist (and will resist "all efforts to validate transgender identity"). However, we must take the discriminator's word for it. We do not know if they have a sincerely held religious belief that prompts them into discriminating, or simply because they are transphobic and hate trans people.

Sanders continues:

> There is reason to doubt whether the new Trump policy will carefully balance the interests of all concerned. The new rules appear to be a political reward to the Christian right, part of Trump's all-important base. They're being spearheaded by former Heritage Foundation activist Roger Severino, who has long promoted the idea that law must favor religious viewpoints over the rights of LGBTQ people.
>
> Health policy making should not be outsourced to Christian conservatives who deny that a person can medically change their gender identity. It does not matter to these conservatives that gender dysphoria is a recognized diagnosis with established treatment protocols. They believe transition-related medical care can be refused because transgender people are, according to an essay in the religious-conservative journal *Public Discourse*, an "absurdity."

He concludes:

> Trump's new policy would empower workers to withhold care because they object to a patient's identity and because such workers believe their religious liberty allows them to denigrate the patient's very being. Government should not place its authority behind religion when it would require a health care organization to deny someone not only care, but basic human dignity.

What is "Discrimination"?

In *When Harry Became Sally* and in in many screeds on the *Heritage Foundation's* website, Ryan T. Anderson argues against adding "sexual orientation and gender identity" to anti-discrimination laws. But, on page 197 of the book in question, he writes:

> If people are being turned away from restaurants or denied basic medical care solely on the basis of a transgender identity, that is real discrimination and it should be addressed appropriately so that people are treated with dignity and respect.

Yet on pages 202 and 203, he argues against trans anti-discrimination laws. He also disses them in a *Heritage Foundation* article. We read:[26]

> Sexual orientation and gender identity (SOGI) antidiscrimination laws are unjustified.

Which is it then? Should trans discrimination be addressed or not? Trans discrimination is certainly real. He writes, "If people are being turned away from restaurants..."

In 2015, Briana Sandy was refused service at Tempe Tavern. We read:[27]

> "All I wanted to do was see a horse race and have a drink," Briana Sandy said.
> But Sandy said she didn't expect what happened.
> "'I can't serve you any drinks,' and I go, 'What? What's the problem?' And she goes, 'We don't serve your kind,' and I'm like, I didn't just hear that. And then all of a sudden, this guy, who was I guess the bouncer, walked up to me and he goes, 'You're going to have to leave,'" she said.

The tavern did not deny it. The tavern posted on the internet, "A person of the LGBTQ community came into the bar and was denied service."

Much to Dr. Anderson's chagrin, and despite his desire to ban trans anti-discrimination laws, trans anti-discrimination laws do exist in some places in the USA. Here is a reason why:[28]

> Transgender Law Center assisted two transgender women in Los Angeles who were wrongfully asked to leave a restaurant in Burbank in October. While eating dinner, the two women, Jennifer Reid and Victoria Rose were approached by the restaurant's manager and asked to leave, allegedly because their clothing was not appropriate for a "family restaurant." The women rightly believed that they were being targeted because of their gender identity and contacted TLC for information about the law and their rights.

The article continues:

> Jenny and Victoria's experience is an example of how transgender and gender nonconforming people often experience discrimination in their communities when accessing public accommodations, including being refused service, being treated differently than their non-transgender peers, or being victims to harmful verbal and physical violence when simply trying to carry out their daily activities.

The TCNE 2015 US Transgender Survey of 27,715 transgender respondents states that nearly one-third (31%) of respondents who visited a store, restaurant, hotel, or theater where the staff knew or thought they were transgender were mistreated because of their gender identity or expression.[29]

Let's move on to medical care. Anderson writes, "If people are...denied basic medical care solely on the basis of a transgender identity..."

In *Doctors Refuse to Treat Trans Patients More Often Than You Think*, Keren Landman writes:[30]

> On January 18, the US Department of Health and Human Services proposed new regulations and announced the creation of a "Conscience and Religious Freedom Division," both focused on supporting healthcare providers who refuse to perform certain healthcare services on religious or moral grounds.
>
> "Not more of this shit," thought Marian, the mother of a transmasculine teen named Julian who lives in rural Georgia. (Marian chose to withhold her and Julian's full names due to safety concerns.)
>
> In 2016, Marian said a nurse practitioner in a local supermarket's walk-in health care clinic had repeatedly and intentionally misgendered Julian while administering his testosterone injection, asking, "What kind of a doctor would prescribe this to a girl?" As far as Marian could see, the provider's disgust was evident—and a week later, the provider called to inform her there would be no staff available to perform the procedure in the clinic for Julian's next injection, suggesting they instead try a different clinic in a nearby town.
>
> While the nurse practitioner's reasons for refusing Julian care were ambiguous, her actions were legal; according to Georgia state law, a pharmacist may "refuse to fill any prescription based on professional judgment or ethical or moral beliefs."
>
> Marian wasn't taking any chances; instead of risking another refusal, she opted for the 200-mile round trip to Julian's doctor's office in Atlanta.

This is not isolated. A Williams Institute survey of 6,456 self-identified transgender and gender non-conforming adults aged 18 and over states that 60% of those who attempted suicide were refused medical treatment because they were trans.[31]

On page 200 of When Harry Became Sally, Ryan T. Anderson claims that that, regarding medical professionals refusing to treat transgender people for non-trans health issues:

> And there is no evidence...for the claim that this kind of thing "sometimes happens."

Anderson backs this "no evidence" claim with...

...no evidence.

But the *National Transgender Discrimination Survey Report on health and health care,* which provided the health care report from a survey of over 7000 people provides the following statistics:[32]

> Twenty-two percent (22%) of MTF respondents reported having been refused treatment altogether, whereas 19% of FTM respondents did.

They further found that "28% of respondents were subjected to harassment in medical settings."

And let us not forget Tyra Hunter.

In 1995, Tyra Hunter was in an automobile accident. In an analysis, we read:[33]

> Tyra was knocked out by the crash, but by the time the firemen arrived, she was conscious but dazed, and developing airway trouble from teeth knocked into her mouth. Tyra looked female at first glance, but in their initial injury assessment, a fireman discovered Ty's male genitals, uttered the epithets ("This ain't no bitch. It's a n****r. He's got a dick and balls."), and ceased treating her. They failed

to clear her airway for some period of time while they laughed at her as the crowd yelled at them to get to work. Other emergency personnel on scene approached some time later, after treating the other injured passenger. They found Tyra still lying on the grass, gagging and combative, apparently trying to escape the taunting firemen. Supervisor Roulhac then arrived and ordered Ty's airway cleared.

She did eventually arrive at the ER. But she was mostly ignored. She was given a drug to paralyze her (and thus stop complaining), but:

> Tyra's pulse and blood pressure slowly fell, and she suffocated from lack of oxygen in her blood. Dr. Baker testified that the sensation would have been "sheer terror."
> ...she lay there for over half an hour without treatment. She died at 5:20 p.m. Only then did the ER staff insert a chest tube, releasing at least 1500 ccs of blood, as well as air, that had built up in her chest.[34]

Despite Anderson's denial that trans people have been denied health care, it does exist and is not uncommon. They are refused service in restaurants and elsewhere. Anti-transgender activists are not trying to stop this discrimination; they are encouraging it.

When Mike Pence was Governor of Indiana, he signed a law to do just that. In *Indiana Passes Insane Law Giving Restaurants the Right to Refuse Gay Diners*, Khushbu Shah writes:[35]

> Every human must eat, but according to Mike Pence — the governor of Indiana — not every person has the right to eat at a restaurant. In an incredibly discriminatory move, Pence signed into law today a bill that allows businesses — including restaurants, coffee shops, and bars — to turn away customers that are gay, lesbian, and transgender. According to CNN, Pence attempted to justify the move by citing "religious freedom": "The Constitution of the United States

and the Indiana Constitution both provide strong recognition of the freedom of religion but today, many people of faith feel their religious liberty is under attack by government action." How having paying LGBT customers attacks a business owners' freedom of religion is not explained.

Pence is not the only one pushing this. We also read:[36]

Unfortunately, Pence isn't the first politician to use twisted logic to defend "freedom of religion." Earlier this month in an op-ed for the Washington Examiner, Republican Senator James Lankford and Representative Randy Forbes argued that because Chipotle is allowed to remove carnitas from its menu when suppliers don't meet its standards for animal welfare, businesses should be allowed to make decisions — including who they can turn away — based on their religious standards.

On page 197 of When Harry Became Sally, Ryan T. Anderson argues FOR keeping discrimination against LGBT people legal. He writes:

There are no denials of the right to vote, no lynchings, no signs over water fountains saying "Gay" and "Straight."

If Anderson peeked out of his tiny anti-trans echo chamber, he may learn that these very much do exist. Regarding the denial of a right to vote, we read, in *Tea Party Group Targets Trans Voters*:[37]

> A right-wing, Tea Party organization called "True the Vote" is training their volunteer poll watchers to target transgender voters. True the Vote's training manual features a transphobic image that claims transgender people are fraudulent voters and should be denied the right to vote.
>
> NCTE Executive Director Mara Keisling said, "It is disgraceful that True the Vote would try to thug anyone into not voting. True the Vote's true agenda is a shameful attempt to scare trans people away from participating in our democracy."
>
> Until this point, the concerted effort by right-wing, tea party groups to restrict voting rights with new Voter ID laws only inadvertently affected transgender voters. Only days away from Election Day, the discovery of True the Vote's training manual marks a shift by right-wing groups to explicitly target transgender people and deny them a right to vote.

In *States are making it a lot harder for transgender people to vote*, we read:[38]

> Once you think about it, these hurdles are pretty obvious. For example, a trans person's legal name, photo, or gender marker just may not be updated on a legal ID, because state law makes it difficult or impossible to alter that kind of information. So when trans people show up at the polling booth, they may have their identities questioned and denied because their physical appearance doesn't match what their ID says. And that could hinder trans people's ability to vote, or stop them from voting altogether.
>
> This situation is enabled by state laws that are very strict in what kind of ID is required to vote — Texas, for example,

allows a driver's license or other government-issued ID, but not a student ID or bank statement. States can also make it difficult to update the name, photo, or gender marker on government-issued IDs.

According to NCTE, five states have strict voter ID laws *and* make it very difficult or even impossible for trans people to change the gender markers on their IDs: Alabama, Georgia, Kansas, Mississippi, and Tennessee.

The Williams Institute concluded that about 25,000 transgender people could have been disenfranchised in the November 2012 election from nine states alone.[39]

Regarding Anderson's "no lynchings" of trans people, we read the story of Dandara dos Santos:[40]

> The killing of a transgender woman who was beaten, tortured, shot and then bashed on the head with a big stone has horrified and transfixed Brazil, training attention on the violence and discrimination suffered by transgender people in South America's most populous nation...
>
> The grisly video shows Ms. dos Santos sitting on the ground, covered in dust and blood, being kicked in the face, beaten with a plank of wood and forced into a wheelbarrow. According to the authorities, she was later taken to a nearby street, shot twice in the face and then bludgeoned.

In Florida, we read:[41]

> The transgender community and the family of a transgender woman named India Clarke are in mourning after police said she was found apparently beaten to death in a Tampa, Florida, park this past Tuesday morning...
>
> Clarke was discovered with "obvious signs of homicidal violence to the upper body," lying on the ground next to basketball courts at a park by Tampa's University Area Community Center.

These brutal murders of trans people are not that uncommon. We have already read that there were 28 such lynchings in 2017 in the USA. Some are done with incredible hatred. In *Prosecutors seek death penalty in transgender teen's grisly killing*, we read:[42]

> Vrba is charged with first-degree murder in the death of 17-year-old Ally Steinfeld...
>
> Investigators say Steinfeld was stabbed several times, including in the genitals, and her eyes were gouged out and her body set on fire.

What is Transphobia?

Julia Serano defines this rather well.[43]

> So when I just mentioned trans people being harassed on the streets, or denied jobs or housing, most reasonable people would agree that those are examples of transphobia. But transphobia isn't merely the "fear" or "hatred" of transgender people. No, it is best thought of as a double standard that is pervasive in our society, and which presumes that cisgender (that is, non-transgender) bodies, identities, and experiences are valid and the unspoken norm, whereas their transgender counterparts are deemed illegitimate, inauthentic, defective, and suspect in comparison.
>
> This is important to stress, because often the authors of these op-eds and think-pieces will stress how they are "pro-trans" or "trans-friendly," yet they will nevertheless make a statement or express an opinion that clearly reveals that they view trans people's genders to be less valuable or valid than their cis counterparts. In the same way that expressions of sexism, racism, ableism, or homophobia can be subtle and unconscious, the same holds true for expressions of transphobia.

To me, that very well describes the tone of *When Harry Became Sally*.

What Needs to Be Done

Education and advocacy is key, as is voting the Trump administration out of office. His election has emboldened anti-LGBT activists and other hate groups (including Neo-Nazis, the KKK, and White Nationalists) to act on their ideologies.

Anti-trans websites and books are on the rise. These aim to normalize the idea that trans people are delusional, that they kidnap children and force them into sex changes, that they should legally be discriminated against, that they should be denied health care, that they deserve at every turn is scorn, contempt and belittlement, that their very identity should be invalidated, that they are inhuman.

One can take a stand. Write a bad review for a bigoted book and explain your reasons. When a friend, colleague, or family member verbally agrees with the propaganda against trans people, let them know that you do not feel that way. They may come around.

If they are watching a far-right "News" channel, ask nicely if you could change the station. If you can get them to watch a reality-based news program, they may get to know and understand reality rather than propaganda. Indeed, think of it. If all of your news came from stations that dehumanize trans people, you would likely come to believe that it is OK to do so. A fresh, honest look at how trans people really are could be the turning point, yes? It could be so with your friends, too.

The National Center for Transgender Equality (NCTE) lists 52 things that a person can do for transgender rights. They are:[44]

#1: Take a Trans Person to Lunch

#2: Ask your library to carry books that deal positively with trans people

#3: Attend an anti-racism training and put into practice what you learn

#4: Run for Office

#5: Invite your mayor or other elected official to address a trans group or town meeting

#6: Plan an Art Show of Works by Trans Artists

#7: Create and publicize a calendar of local events and encourage people to attend them

#8: Start an online community or a blog that deals with an issue that is important to you

#9: Change the Policy of an Organization You Belong To

#10: Donate money to an organization providing direct services for transgender people

#11: Hold a workshop on how to effectively advocate for yourself when seeking medical care or therapy

#12: Ask Your Local Film Festival to Show Trans Themed Movies and then Go See Them

#13: Support the Day of Silence

#14: Preach or speak at a local community of faith, such as a synagogue, church or mosque

#15: Adopt a Highway

#16: Hold a Trans Pride event in your community

#17: March as a trans contingent in the Gay Pride Parade

#18: Educate a local homeless shelter about how to be trans inclusive

#19: Pass a non-discrimination ordinance in your community

#20: Visit the offices of your congressional representative and educate them about trans issues

#21: Start a local support or education group

#22: Volunteer with an LGBT Advocacy group

#23: Start a Speakers' Bureau

#24: Break a Gender Rule

#25: Make a Restroom More Accessible to Trans People

#26: Locate Support Services

#27: Collaborate with another group on a community project or social event.

#28: Work to Pass a Nondiscrimination Policy at Your Workplace

#29: Connect with PFLAG!

#30 Write a regular column for a publication

#31: Plan to Come out on National Coming Out Day on October 11

#32: Register New Voters!

#33: Fund Scholarships!

#34: Programs for Youth

#35: Know your rights if you are stopped by the police

#36 Get involved in the political process: Volunteer for a Candidate

#37 Plan and conduct a Day of Remembrance event

#38 Support or create a radio show or podcast

#39 Hold a House Party for NCTE or another trans organization

#40 Make Jails Safer for Trans People

#41 Hold a Job Fair

#42 Support a Drag Community Event

#43 Engage Media Coverage of Transgender Issues

#44 Conduct a Community Needs Assessment

#45 Vote!

#46 Start a discussion group on gender related books

#47 Respond to Alerts from Other Organizations

#48 Collect and share stories of discrimination

#49 Set up a training in a hospital, nursing or medical school

#50 Write an op-ed

#51 Help an LGBT organization become more transgender friendly

#52 Make a New Year's Resolution for Transgender Equality

These give one idea per week for one year. The first idea, inviting a trans person to lunch (or dinner, for tea or coffee, or whatever) may allow you to get to actually meet and get to know a trans person. The result may be that you learn that the trans person is indeed human, is not crazy, and is pretty much just like everyone else, with the exception of being born with a gender identity that did not match their assigned sex at birth.

Conclusion

I was asked why I wrote this book. Why open myself to transphobia and bigotry? It is this: when I read *When Harry Became Sally*, I was flabbergasted by the one-sided anti-trans statements constantly being made. The author rarely went outside of the anti-trans echo chamber. And when he did, such as with the Dhejne study, he appears to misrepresent it in ways to draw a reader to a very different conclusion than the original science showed. The book appears to be designed to draw readers away from science by mainstream and caring professionals and instead aims them toward hard-right and dangerous philosophy and anti-LGBT politics.

The book became a bestseller. Positive reviews on Amazon state, "the truth!", "balanced and thoughtful", "with compassion", "breath of reality", "full of scientific reality," "unbiased", etc.

That is disheartening. Too many people are believing the book. The anti-transgender movement has gone too far, and transgender people are being harmed. People need to stand up and share actual truth.

The main point that Ryan T. Anderson seems to be stressing in the book is that transgender people should be denied medical care and civil rights. He backs this up with opinions of anti-transgender activists within his echo chamber.

But if we go outside of that small group, we see that most professionals state and show that medical care is not only beneficial but often necessary.

Surgery regret does (rarely) occur. There can be rare complications. Not just with transgender surgery, but any surgery. If one patient dies from a heart transplant, should we ban it completely, even though many lives would be saved if we allow the surgery for qualified patients?

Similarly, if we find a few, out of thousands of people who have had transgender surgery, had a degree of regret, should we ban medical intervention completely, even though many lives could be saved if we allow it for qualified patients?

He maintains that "biology isn't bigotry" in efforts to prevent medical care and allow discrimination. Yet we see that science shows that there are physical causes for transgenderism, and it affects the brain. And the brain is "biology."

I would like to counter "biology isn't bigotry" (indeed, biology supports the fact that being transgendered is not a choice) with "science isn't stupid."

I would further argue that "biology *is* bigotry." The idea that "Sally is Trans; that is a biological fact; therefore, it should be just fine to discriminate against *him* (and misgender and disrespect Sally)" *is* bigotry. What if someone said, "race isn't bigotry," "religion isn't bigotry," or "national origin isn't bigotry"?

Nearly all professionals who treat transgendered patients agree that their condition is not their choice and that medical care is often necessary, and their opinions and research is based on science rather than anti-trans political ideology.

Anderson appears to have never engaged in conversation or other intercourse with a single transgendered individual. Yet the book appears to be one of authority on trans issues.

This treatment of transgendered individuals as an abstract concept, rather than real people, to be written about with the apparent motive to support laws against them, is especially telling.

We have also seen that others in the echo chamber are similar. We have seen that Paul Hruz, the "expert" witness in a transgender law case, has not treated any transgender patients, patients with gender dysphoria, conducted peer-reviewed research about gender identity, transgender people, or gender dysphoria; and is not a psychiatrist, a psychologist, nor mental health care provider *of any kind*.[1]

Rather than discuss the success of a single happy transitioner, of which there are thousands, he focuses only on five stories of detransitioners (plus Walt) that he found on the internet. In a review by Tina Madison White, we see this in an analogy. She writes:[2]

> There are 400,000 priests in the world. Imagine that you want to understand them. Would you turn to a book that bases its conclusions from the experiences of five priests who left the church? Would you consider these five a reliable basis for understanding the 400,000? Would you consider it respectful of the 400,000?

There are alternatives to the anti-trans echo chamber. I hope that this book is one. Not only have I ventured outside of the echo chamber and shared scores of actual research, but I have actually reached out to trans people— I have worked with and met hundreds of transgendered individuals. I have been with them from pre-transition to post surgery.

I have held them in my arms as they cried because of the overwhelming angst that their condition pressed upon them. I have held them as they cried with joy after they transitioned and were finally happy.

I need to let them be acknowledged and heard.

Is the Anti-Trans Moment Here to Stay?

Americans across the country made it obvious, through the power of the purse, that North Carolina's "bathroom bill" was unacceptable.

The bill, known as HB2 or Hate Bill 2, was aimed at keeping transgender people out of certain public facilities. It was rushed through the North Carolina Senate and the North Carolina House of Representatives in one day (23 March 2016) and was signed by the Governor that night.[3]

Many companies reacted in favor of civil rights, and changed plans for doing business with the state, including PayPal, which announced that they were cancelling their expansion into Charlotte. Deutche Bank also canceled their planned expansion of their NC offices. Dozens of other companies did so as well, including those in the film industry.[4]

The NBA, NCAA, NFL and ESPN's X Games have spoken against the law, reconsidering plans to host future sporting events in North Carolina.[5]

Musicians refused to play there. Several states and municipalities banned publicly-funded travel to the state.

One month later, Time Warner Cable News North Carolina estimated that House Bill 2 had to date cost North Carolina more than 1750 jobs and more than $77 million.[6] The Associated Press estimated that House Bill 2 would cost the state US$3.76 billion over twelve years.[7]

This backlash against bigotry cost the governor his job. The Democrat who replaced him, Roy Cooper, signed a bill that removed the bathroom restrictions.

Texas attempted to enact its own bathroom bill, SB6.[8] It would demand a fine of $1,000 for the first visit to a restroom and $10,000 for the second.

A study commissioned by the San Antonio Area Tourism Council showed that Texas could lose $3.3 Billion per year in tourism alone.[9]

The bill has not passed.

A Pew Research survey showed that a narrow majority (51%) feel that transgender people should be able to use the restroom that matches the gender with which they currently identify, while 46% say they should be required to use the restroom of their birth gender.[10] They also state that young adults (18-29) are far more likely than their elders to take the position that transgender people should be allowed to use restrooms that correspond to their current gender identify.

Another Pew Research survey states:[11]

> About four-in-ten adults (39%) say society has not gone far enough in accepting people who are transgender, while 32% say society has gone too far and 27% say it has been about right.

They also show that the younger generations are less likely to believe that someone's gender must equal their assigned sex. This hopefully suggests that transphobia will decrease as the generations age.

A popular method of punishment for transgender people, especially children, is to subject them to conversion therapy. But we have seen just how horrible that can be, often leading to suicide (a "statistic" for activists to further use against the trans population).

And people are pushing back. Conversion therapy against children is now illegal in ten states.[12] 36 municipalities plus the District of Columbia also ban it.

Maryland may become the 11th state to ban it. In *LGBT 'Conversion Therapy' Is Dying a Quick Death Across America. Good.*, Samantha Allen writes:[13]

> A conversion therapy ban in Maryland, as Into reported, is basically a done deal now that it has passed the House of Delegates.

As Washington Post columnist Karen Tumulty highlighted, one of the most moving speakers in support of the impending Maryland ban was bisexual Republican delegate Meagan Simonaire who shared a story about a girl who underwent conversion therapy and experienced "significant pain, self-loathing, and deep depression"—all before disclosing that she herself was the subject of the story.

Another action that is in the right direction is the fact that Johns Hopkins resumed medical care for transgendered patients. Trans surgeries were halted in 1979 due to the ideology of McHugh and Mayer that trans people were simply mentally ill. *In Johns Hopkins to resume gender-affirming surgeries after nearly 40 years*, we read:[14]

> Earlier this month, the heads of Johns Hopkins Medicine issued a letter to their colleagues addressing increasing scrutiny on the institution. One of its faculty members, Paul McHugh, has become the face of anti-transgender advocacy, propping up junk science to justify rejecting transgender identities. McHugh's latest "special report" in *The New Atlantis*, co-authored with Lawrence Mayer, another Johns Hopkins professor, challenged basic premises about the nature of LGBT identities by cherry-picking studies and sounding anti-LGBT dogwhistles.
>
> ...the letter then outlines an institutional commitment to LGBT nondiscrimination and affirmation that directly contradicts the doubts they raised in their report. The list includes expanding benefits to cover transgender health services ("including surgical procedures") and a plan to develop "new paths for our institutions to further approaches to evidence-based, patient-centered care for LGBT individuals."
>
> ...We have committed to and will soon begin providing gender-affirming surgery as another important element of our overall care program, reflecting careful consideration

over the past year of best practices and the appropriate provision of care for transgender individuals.

Science has overcome ideology.

And just recently, New Hampshire stood up to transphobia and outlawed trans discrimination. This was done by a GOP-controlled state legislature (both houses) *and* a Republican Governor. In Slate's *The Triumph of Transgender Rights in New Hampshire Is a GOP Rebuke to Mike Pence and Jeff Sessions,* we read:[15]

> This bipartisan triumph for transgender equality contrasts sharply with Donald Trump's unrelenting assault on transgender rights. Indeed, it should be been seen as a rebuke to his persistent attacks on LGBTQ Americans. The Trump administration has revoked federal guidance protecting transgender students, employees, and homeless people. It is poised to attempt to repeal nondiscrimination protections for transgender patients under the Affordable Care Act. And, of course, it is striving to ban open transgender military service by arguing that trans people are mentally unstable deviants. Vice President Mike Pence and Attorney General Jeff Sessions are the driving force behind the onslaught: Pence intervened behind the scenes to overrule Secretary of Defense James Mattis' support for trans service, while Sessions has issued a stream of directives designed to undermine LGBTQ rights under federal law.

The tide may turn eventually, and our culture may learn to respect the reality of gender identity. But anti-trans activists have deep pockets and numerous websites and "News" organizations are working constantly to turn the public against its LGBT citizens.

A Plan of Action

As with other forms of bigotry, those who practice it are not generally looked upon favorably by history. But we should not wait until they need to explain to their grandchildren why they mistreated good people. We can act now. If you read a book or article where the author intends to bamboozle you into thinking that trans people are less than human, or should be denied medical coverage or civil rights, and back up their balderdash with endnotes of works by McHugh, Meyer, Cretella, or any type of crackpot; call them out on it. Likely, their motives for writing such rigmarole were not pure.

This book, a parody of *When Harry Became Sally,* is an action against transphobia. Due to the points already made, I cannot see how *When Harry Became Sally* is anything but an action *for* propagating transphobia, and is (IMHO) meant to be dangerous. It is (and other works are) dividing citizens into "us and them", with "them" being LGB and *especially* T. Such works are already being used to justify keeping trans people out of restrooms, out of the military, and to be denied medical care.

But he is not alone. Many people are being pulled into the anti-transgender movement, drawn by a bombardment of anti-trans articles and opinions on far-right websites.

Do not let them hoodwink you.

But as we advocate for truth, we should be careful not stigmatize those that have fallen for their hype. Educate them. And foremost, do not ignore it. As the saying goes, *remember, it didn't start with gas chambers. It started with politicians who divided the people "us vs. them". It started with intolerance and hate speech. When people stopped caring, became desensitized, and turned a blind-eye, it became a slippery slope to genocide.*

If this seems alarming, it is. It is important that we realize that it (the anti-transgender moment) is dangerous.

When someone, especially a politician or author, dehumanizes anyone, whether they be a refugee, an immigrant, a member of the LGBT citizenry, or *anyone* "different," and seeks to deny them basic human rights, take a stand. Ask them to imagine walking in their shoes. If they claim that their dehumanization of the minority group is due to a "sincere religious belief," ask them if they have heard of "do unto others as you would have them do to you."

If you see a trans person being attacked. It is OK to help them or seek help. Too often, trans people do get physically attacked, yet bystanders record the attack on their phones for entertainment. Please do not be such a bystander. Please do not be the attacker.

If someone is being subjected to conversion therapy or other such mistreatment. Try to help them. Mistreatment for gender dysphoria can lead to deep depression and even suicide. Share with them the Trevor Project hotline. It is 866-488-7386.[16] The website states:

> Our trained counselors are here to support you 24/7. If you are a young person in crisis, feeling suicidal, or in need of a safe and judgment free place to talk, call the Trevor Lifeline.

Let us help reduce the suicide statistics for transgender youth and adults.

What's at stake in the anti-transgender moment are human beings, especially the most vulnerable— transgender people, children included. If anti-trans activists succeed in their agenda, transgender people will continue to be further marginalized, physically attacked, and denied civil rights. Their well-beings will deteriorate; suicides will increase.

This does not have to happen. Everyone can have a role in treating each other with compassion and respect.

Afterword: The Challenge

In writing this book, I set out to correct misleading points made in Ryan T. Anderson's book. I also took up his challenges. The first was:[1]

> Boylan claims I wrote "a book that suggests that transgender people are crazy, and that what we [people who identify as transgender] deserve at every turn is *scorn, contempt, and belittlement*."
> **Good luck finding a single line from my book to back up either claim**. I wrote nothing of the sort...

First, and in many cases, Anderson deliberately misgenders trans people at every opportunity. We have seen that this is, if not deliberately malicious, entirely disrespectful. One cannot deliberately misgender someone and claim respect. Thus, this can clearly be construed as **scorn**.

Intentional misgendering is *never* respectable or acceptable. It is the same as using a racial slur. I have read posts by anti-trans activists who claim that they do not disrespect people who have gender dysphoria yet will intentionally misgender them because "it is the truth!" A racist could say the same about his victims and use a slur, claiming that it is "the truth." It is not the truth. Slurs are not "the truth." They are invidious and offensive. They are not used with respect but with **contempt**. It is the same with deliberate misgendering. It is always a slur.

Next, we see that he argues against allowing a transgender child to transition, even if the child is an insistent, persistent, DSM-5-diagnosed gender dysphoric

171

trandgendered child whose life would be so much better if they were allowed to go through the proper puberty for them. The stated desire to prevent this beneficial therapy can certainly be construed as **contemptible**, as was his commentary in defense of that:[2]

> Parents in Ohio lost custody of their 17-year-old daughter Friday because a judge ruled that she should be allowed to receive therapy, including testosterone therapy, to identify as a boy.
> Without commenting on the specifics of this case...

Not only did he deliberately misgenders the boy, but "Without commenting on the specifics of this case" he slammed the court's decision to remove a child from parents who were abusing him while deliberately leaving the abuse part out. I would assume that Anderson would not have any qualms about removing a cisgendered child from abusive parents. But a transgendered child? How about Kirk? We read that the father "spanked" Kirk "so hard that he had welts up and down his back and on his buttocks," by order of the conversion therapist. Kirk later took his (her, rather) life. It appears that the idea here is to let the parents abuse the trans child; trans lives are worth less than others. That is the definition of **belittlement**.

We know that conversion therapy is dangerous child abuse. We have read stories of its victims. Yet, on page 143, about which he writes:

> Apart from the alleged lack of success, what could make that kind of treatment unethical?

What could make child abuse unethical?! Seriously! Oh, wait; these are trans kids in question; their lives don't matter as much. What is worse is his joke about it on Twitter. He tweeted:[3]

"Conversion" therapy? That's the therapy where you block puberty and give testosterone to girls in an attempt to convert them into boys? Or do you mean something else?

How could he be so **contemptible** and flippant about a type of abuse that can lead young people to kill themselves? And doing so while **belittling** what is often the best treatment for a transgendered child? Boylan and Ford have a point. That was quite disrespectful of Dr. Anderson.

Nowhere in the book is there any evidence that he ever reached out to a happily-transitioned trans person. He treated them as hypothetical creatures, abstract concepts, not real people, the "others" rather than "us", not worth the bother. That is another classic case of **belittlement**. Does he avoid trans people because he thinks that they are icky? Why?

And in treating trans lives as such, he vehemently argues against trans discrimination being made illegal, and argues that it should remain legal, and that laws should explicitly say so. He especially does so in Chapter 8. That is **scorn, contempt, *and* belittlement**. He even suggests that no trans discrimination as such exists. On page 197, he writes

> If people are being turned away from restaurants or denied basic medical care solely on the basis of a transgender identity, that is real discrimination and it should be addressed appropriately so that people are treated with dignity and respect.

Yet he then argues against addressing it at all. And we saw that a large percentage of transgendered people routinely get discriminated against at restaurants and elsewhere, even hospitals. And not just for transgender-related medical care, but non-trans care. Yet he writes, on page 200, regarding trans people getting denied non-trans medical care"

And there is no evidence...for the claim that this kind of thing "sometimes happens."

We have seen that they is; plenty of evidence has already been discussed. On page 197, he writes:

There are no denials of the right to vote, no lynchings,

Yet we read that trans disenfranchisement is rather widespread. And, yes, there are lynchings, too.

The second challenge was:

Ford immediately jumped to Boylan's defense on Twitter, writing: "You call them mentally ill." I replied: "Simple. **Please quote the passage where I 'call them mentally ill.'** You can't quote that passage because it doesn't exist."

Let's get started. On page 95, he quotes McHugh:

"This intensely felt sense of being transgendered constitutes a mental disorder..."

He writes, on page 96:

The "disordered assumption: of those who identify as the opposite sex, he says, is similar to the faulty assumption of those who suffer from anorexia nervosa, who believe themselves to be overweight when in fact they are dangerously thin.

Mental disorder; disordered assumption. Those sound like accusations of craziness to me. A transgendered person does not necessarily have a disordered assumption. They rather often *know* that their gender identity is opposite to the sex that they were assigned at birth. And comparing gender dysphoria to anorexia is rude to both trans people and anorexic people.

He immediately continues:

> Dr. Josephson describes the phenomenon as a "delusion," which in psychiatry refers to "a fixed, false belief which is held despite clear evidence to the contrary."

Where I come from, calling someone delusional is calling them mentally ill. He continues with the bogus "false beliefs" motif on the following page (page 97):

> Mental health professionals must not simply help people survive with whatever beliefs they happen to hold, but to help people accept the truth, as they work through the deeper issues beneath the false beliefs.

The truth is that they do not have a false belief about their gender identity. He continues on that same page with:

> ...false beliefs...false assumptions...false beliefs.

What part of "false belief" does Anderson not understand? A trans person may indeed *know* that their gender identity is opposite to the sex that they were assigned at birth. That is *not* a delusion. As explained earlier, they are born that way. This whole thing reminds me of a child when they stick their fingers in their ears and say, "La la la; I can't hear you."

On page 110, he writes, regarding transwomen, that they are either gay and seek surgery to have sex with men, or that they are perverts. He also suggests that these pervs enjoy masochistic activities such as autoerotic asphyxia. The point, I assume, is to insult transwomen and get the reader to hate them. And to label them as crazy. And to insult them out of disrespect.

On page 104, he compares gender dysphoria to someone claiming to be a bat. That sounds a lot like an accusation of mental illness to me.

On page 114, he states that someone who has had gender affirming surgery may be "believing and living out a falsehood." Crazy, huh?

On page 116, he states:

Recall that a delusion, in psychiatric terms, is a "fixed, false belief which is held despite clear evidence to the contrary." If this concept applies to anorexia and to body dysmorphic disorder, why should it not apply to gender identity disorder?

There is that *trans people are delusional* again, along with the false equivalence between gender dysphoria (once called gender identity disorder) and anorexia or body dysmorphic disorder.

On page 209, he compares someone with gender dysphoria to someone believing that they are a great horned owl or a Russian princess.

In all, it sure appears to me that Anderson is claiming that people with gender dysphoria are delusional and *mentally ill*, and deserve, at every turn, *scorn, contempt, and belittlement*.

The final challenge was:

> Boylan claims my book is "abundant in junk science," but couldn't point to anything in particular that I got wrong.

First, *When Harry Became Sally* does appear to be pseudoscience, that is, the author appears to have "sought only confirming evidence while ignoring disconfirming cases."[4]

Dr. Anderson works for the anti-LGBT Heritage Foundation.[5] As such, were he to write a book about trans issues, he would not go against his employer and write a book favorable to trans citizens; the conclusion of the book would thus be decided before the first words were typed.

It looks like pseudoscience was used for the references. Dr. Anderson relied heavily on a small group of anti-trans activists who happen to have doctoral degrees. Mainly, they do not treat trans patients, but are outspoken. Their opinions (right or wrong, and usually wrong) fill the book.

What is lacking are the numerous actual studies about trans patients. They tell a different story—one that shows that trans people are not delusional, and that they benefit from medical treatment.

When non-biased sources were used, such as the Dhejne study, it was misrepresented, as we have seen. The purpose of the misrepresentation seems to be to steer the reader into believing that surgery makes things worse, and that their risk of suicide *increases* due to said surgery. This was most egregious when he cited this same study in his highly misleading, *Sex Reassignment Doesn't Work. Here Is the Evidence*:[6]

> Ten to 15 years after surgical reassignment, *the suicide rate of those who had undergone sex-reassignment surgery* **rose** *to 20 times that of comparable peers. (emphasis added)

The surgery made the suicide rate *rise*?! That just isn't true (and I am sure that he knows it). We saw in the 2006 study by G. De Cuypere et al. entitled *Long-term follow-up: Psychosocial outcome of Belgian transsexuals after sex reassignment surgery*,[7] that the suicide attempt-rate dropped significantly—from 29.3% to 5.1%.

Also egregious is Dr. Anderson's and his circle of activists' utilization of propaganda from hate groups, such as the Family Research Council, American Family Association, Alliance Defending Freedom, and especially ACPeds. Would it make sense, if one wanted to write about African American civil rights, to use propaganda from the KKK? If you are writing a book about Jewish history, would you use Nazi literature? It is the same here. Using anti-trans hate groups' codswallop would, and IMHO, did, produce a very biased, nonscientific, and misleading book.

Let us look at some of the junk science in the book.

There was much use of Mayer's and McHugh's opinion piece, *Sexuality and Gender* published by *The New Atlantis*. It has 26 pages of endnotes and citations, but that is meaningless. The conclusion is just an opinion that does not reflect the discussion or the studies that they chose to include.

The Gender Identity section concludes with:[8]

> The scientific evidence summarized suggests we take a skeptical view toward the claim that sex-reassignment procedures provide the hoped for benefits or resolve the underlying issues that contribute to elevated mental health risks among the transgender population.

Well, that's just wrong. The scientific evidence readily available and in this book and its endnotes show differently. There are at least 85 studies that show that sex reassignment surgery (gender affirming surgery) helps.[9]

There were three studies discussed in the gender section of the *New Atlantis* opinion piece immediately before their conclusion. The first was the Dhejne study,[10] which was misrepresented like it was in *When Harry Became Sally*:

> In summary, this study suggests that sex-reassignment surgery may not rectify the comparatively poor health outcomes associated with transgender populations in general.

Dhejne herself has, as we have read, made it clear that that is not what her study showed.

The next study was one by Annette Kuhn, et al.[11] It was an apples and oranges comparison of 51 post-op trans patients who have had *at least six* surgeries to 49 cisgendered people who have had at least one pelvic surgery but *less than six* surgeries. The *New Atlantis* opinion piece stated:

> This study found considerably lower general life satisfaction in post-surgical transsexuals as compared with females who had at least one pelvic surgery in the past. The postoperative

transsexuals reported lower satisfaction with their general quality of health and with some of the personal, physical, and social limitations they experienced with incontinence that resulted as a side effect of the surgery.

Considerably lower?! If we look at Table 2 of the report, we see that only physical limitation and personal limitation are statistically different from the cisgender controls. General health, role limitation, emotions, sleep, incontinence, and symptom severity were not statistically different (to determine a statistical difference, one looks at the "p value." If the value is below 0.05, then one can say that there is a statistical, or significant, difference between the groups). Thus, the *New Atlantis* piece misrepresents that study as well. By using this on page 103 of the Harry book, Anderson misconstrued the same study in the same manner.

Finally, they discussed a 2009 study by Mohammad Hassan Murad, et al. that evaluated 28 studies with a total of 1833 patients.[12] They found that 80% of individuals with GID reported significant improvement in gender dysphoria after surgery and hormone therapy.

That study shows that the vast majority greatly benefited from HRT and surgery, which is contrary to the specious "conclusions" that Meyer and McHugh are trying to hoodwink the public into believing. They did take the opportunity to call the study "very low quality evidence," but one might wonder why a pseudoscience "study" would include disconfirming cases. I suspect that it may be to counter critics. Imagine:

CRITIC: "How could you come to your conclusion? Haven't you even heard of the Murad study [or a number of other studies showing that surgery helps]?"

MEYER or MCHUGH: "We have! We included it! It was one of many that we considered [and ignored]!"

In the same manner, I could write a 150-page report on the shape of the earth, complete with 30 pages of endnotes and citations, utilizing studies from NASA, geologists and physicists, and cartographic surveys. I could then conclude that the earth was a pancake-like disk resting on three elephants, which in turn stand on a giant tortoise that flies through the cosmos. And, like the *New Atlantis* "study," come to the conclusion before I even started the report. The New Atlantis "study" is no less junk science than the proposed Discworld "study."

In the same paragraph where they present the Murad study showing that showed that surgery gave significant improvement, being the paragraph just before their conclusion where they ignore it (and other studies showing how surgery is a good thing), they whine about the following:

> None of the studies included the bias-limiting measure of randomization (that is, in none of the studies were sex-reassignment procedures assigned randomly to some patients but not to others).

This is nearly unbelievably callous. They are suggesting that qualified patients be denied life-saving transgender surgery so that they can be used as control subjects. That would be incredibly cruel. And it again shows how the activists view trans people as abstract concepts, less than human. In clinical trials, consent is given by subjects that they may receive a placebo drug. But consent from a trans person who has finally been given the OK for gender confirmation surgery to be randomly denied said surgery is highly unlikely. The denial would need to be done against the patients will. It appears that this is what they propose.

Would doctors randomly deny a bone marrow or kidney transplant to qualified patients who have a match and are ready for surgery, just to see how worse off their lives would be than those chosen for the life-saving surgeries? Of course not. But, for transgendered people, OK—their lives are less worthy. To me, that is the ultimate insult in the junk science of the *New Atlantis* "study."

But it is not just me. Let us see what others have found:

Mary Beth Maxwell, HRC Vice President for Research, Training, and Programs stated:[13]

Paul McHugh's writings continue to dangerously undermine the safety, security and wellbeing of LGBTQ people, and particularly transgender youth, across the country. McHugh's junk science is still being referenced in legislative and legal battles despite the fact that Paul McHugh has no academic expertise in either gender or sexual orientation, and actively avoids publishing any of his anti-LGBTQ pieces in peer-reviewed journals. Policy makers, informed citizens and parents deserve to know that this is junk science and personal opinion - not at all in the mainstream of current medical and academic research and not endorsed by Johns Hopkins regardless of how McHugh uses his title to suggest credibility or expertise.

In an introduction to a [very well worth watching] video, *How anti-LGBTQ activists are leveraging junk science to advance their agenda*, where Dr. Tonia Poteat debunks the misleading "alternative facts" peddled by McHugh's and Anderson's bubble, especially the *New Atlantis* junk science "study," we read:[14]

Paul McHugh's junk science misrepresents and mischaracterizes existing medical and scientific research. His work is being used to target and discriminate against LGBTQ people across the country. The harm is real, but his science is not. And it's time to call it out.

LGBTQ health expert Dr. Tonia Poteat joins HRC Foundation National Press Secretary Sarah McBride to debunk many of the dangerous myths peddled by McHugh and explain an essential part of the scientific review process he circumvents.

In Undark, regarding the *New Atlantis* "study," we have:[15]

McHugh has received substantial opposition from researchers and clinicians who argue that at best, he engages in a selective reading of the scientific literature, which has continued to uncover compelling evidence that both gender dysphoria and sexual orientation have biological origins. Advocates for LGBTQ rights, meanwhile, suspect McHugh's claims are driven less by science than by pure bias...

It should be noted at the outset that neither McHugh nor Mayer specializes in sexuality or LGBTQ health. Their report also was not peer reviewed, and it contains no original research...

Jack Drescher, a psychiatrist and psychoanalyst who helped write the section on gender for the most recent edition of the American Psychiatric Association's Diagnostic and Statistical Manual of Mental Disorders, made a similarly pragmatic point. "Does his report actually offer alternatives?" he asked. "Because I don't know of anybody who's discovered a way to actually talk a transgender person out of their gender dysphoria.

...Chris Beyrer, an epidemiologist who specializes in LGBTQ health issues at Johns Hopkins and a vocal critic of McHugh, was more blunt: "It's sort of the usual junk science, cherry-picking data, outdated theories," he said...

"If somebody were putting forward the intellectual inferiority of women compared to men, or blacks are inferior to whites, it would be hard to argue that they had the academic freedom to do that," Beyrer told me. "That's junk science. And that's how it feels from an LGBT perspective."

And we should not forget that Johns Hopkins faculty publicly disavowed[16] the junk "study" and that nearly 600 professionals signed[17] a letter stating that the *New Atlantis* report "does not represent prevailing expert consensus opinion about sexual orientation or gender identity related research or clinical care."

In several places (pages 96, 97, 114, 115, 116, 125, and 131), Ryan T. Anderson quotes the opinions of Michelle Cretella, president of the extremist anti-LGBT hate group ACPeds.[18] And as mentioned, he also quotes several other anti-LGBT hate groups. Propaganda by hate groups told specifically to harm a minority group, to promote special political agendas? That is automatic junk science. And there seems to be a lot of it in *When Harry Became Sally.*

When Harry Became Sally may have been meant to be the ultimate blue pill for anti-trans activists and followers, lulling them into believing that transphobia is just. One can read it and comfortably say, "We don't hate trannies; but we do read that they are delusional, are not worthy of medical treatment or civil rights protections, and deserve disrespect."

But from those with actual compassion for transgendered people, who know them, who do not shy away from actual studies, Anderson's book can clearly be read as one that transgendered people deserve at every turn is *scorn, contempt, and belittlement,* and that they are considered to be *mentally ill.* That it is full of *junk science* seems clear as well.

That the book is full of junk science seems not just intentional, but required. In order to write a book conforming to an anti-trans agenda, the sources selected would need to be biased and not necessarily based on real science. And his sources were people who have little or no experience in treating transgender patients, but do have and voice anti-trans opinions. These opinions are thus the sources for an authoritative-sounding, but highly-biased, book.

We should, however, give Dr. Anderson credit for the book. It is an effective (in my opinion) work of anti-trans propaganda. It can and is being used as an "authoritative" piece "showing" that trans people should be denied medical treatment, civil rights, and respect.

His book should not, however, be thought of as an educational book on transgenderism. The predetermined results of the book are far from reality.

Perhaps this book could be a red pill, showing that the reality is that trans people are blatantly mistreated, disrespected, misunderstood, and are real human beings, deserving of medical treatment and civil rights. They are like other people—doctors, lawyers, scientists, engineers, machinists, teachers, authors, and whatever type of employment that you yourself may have.

They are also people tossed out of their homes by parents that read and believe anti-trans propaganda. Disrespected, impoverished, murdered, and discriminated against because of the condition with which they were born. These people do not deserved disrespect or abuse. They deserve compassion and respect (and medical care).

The Challenge

Now that I have met Ryan T. Anderson's challenges, I would like to offer him a challenge. I would like to suggest that he peeps his head outside of the echo chamber bubble of people who seem to have vested interests masquerading as moral principles, and read some real science on gender dysphoria. He would learn that the opinions of his anti-trans colleagues are quite in the minority, and that medical care for gender dysphoria (children included) is good, not evil. But I won't hold my breath. I will, however, challenge the readers of *When Harry Became Sally* to read pertinent literature outside of the anti-trans bubble.

Instead, for Anderson, I will offer something else. We have seen that there is no evidence that Ryan T. Anderson has ever knowingly engaged in a discussion with a happily transitioned trans person (happily transitioned are the vast majority). He has met many trans people that he did not realize were trans, no doubt. That man that he passed as the man was exiting a restroom as he was entering; the one whom Anderson admired his beard? He once had a girl's name. And that nice woman that he met and chatted with at the airport? Yes; trans. Would he have recoiled in horror had he known their pasts? I simply don't know.

One thing that we do know is that, for trans people, familiarity breeds acceptance. A Pew Research survey showed that:[19]

> People who say they personally know someone who is transgender are more likely than those who do not to say society has not gone far enough in accepting transgender people. About half (52%) of those who know someone who is transgender say this, compared with 31% of those who don't know a transgender person.

So, here is my challenge to Ryan T. Anderson:

Have dinner in a public restaurant with at least one happily transitioned trans person (how about making it a party and invite three or four?). Have some drinks with them (we know that you like to drink[20]), and some good food and plenty of conversation. Get to know at least one happily transitioned trans person. You may learn that they are not to be feared or hated. You may gain some friends. You may also gain a fresh new look at the issue of gender dysphoria and the people that it affects.

Cheers!

Acknowledgements

There are hundreds of individuals who contributed their time and efforts in sharing information about transgender issues online, in books, in personal interviews, chats, and in pubs over a few drinks.

I thank all those that endured transition so that they could successfully resolve gender dysphoria and then wrote about it so that others could learn from it, especially those that I mentioned in Chapter 3.

I thank the scientists and clinicians who researched transgender outcomes without bias and shared their results. I thank the doctors that treated transgender patients. Your patients are indebted to you. And we are all indebted to the World Professional Association for Transgender Health for setting up guidelines for helping patients get treated properly.

Special thanks go to those that stand for the rights of LGBT+ people, via voting, letting their views be known, writing about the issues, giving speeches and presentations, giving money to good causes, etc. This also includes those that are simply kind to a fellow human who happens to be LGBT+ and gives them human dignity.

And for good causes, I would like to thank Mara Keisling and the entire team at the National Center for Transgender Equality (NCTE). $0.50 from each book sold goes to NCTE.

Notes

PREFACE

1. Jennifer Finney Boylan, The New York Times, "It's Not a Disaster Movie. It's Reality." https://www.nytimes.com/ 2018/02/27/opinion/transgender-rights.html (accessed 22 April 2018).
2. Ryan T. Anderson, The Heritage Foundation, "A New York Times Writer's Reckless Hit Piece on My Transgender Book," https://www.heritage.org/gender/commentary/ new-york-times-writers-reckless-hit-piece-my-transgender -book (accessed 22 April 2018).

INTRODUCTION

1. Jessica Green, Pink News, "5,000-year-old 'transgender' skeleton discovered," https://www.pinknews.co.uk/ 2011/04/06/5000-year-old-transgender-skeleton- discovered/ (accessed 22 April 2018).
2. Sonali Gupta, India.com, "The History of Hijras—South Asias Transsexual and Transgender Community," http://www.india.com/lifestyle/the-history-of-hijras- south-asias-transsexual-and-transgender-community- 540754/ (accessed 22 April 2018).
3. Ibid.
4. Andy Kang. GLAAD, "India's census counts transgender population for first time" https://www.glaad.org/blog/

indias-census-counts-transgender-population-first-time (accessed 22 April 2018).

5. Rachael Vaughan, The Ethnopsychology Blog, "Two Spirit People: Gender and Transgender in Native American Tradition" http://ethnopsychology-blog.blogspot.com/2011/12/two-spirit-people-gender-and.html (accessed 22 April 2018).

6. Alexis Mijatovic, Out History, "A Brief Biography of Elagabalus: the transgender ruler of Rome," http://outhistory.org/exhibits/show/tgi-bios/elagabalus (accessed 22 April 2018).

7. Ibid.

8. Ibid.

9. Trans Media Watch, "A Trans Timeline," http://www.transmediawatch.org/timeline.html (accessed 22 April 2018).

10. Vincent Garza, Ursa Major Monthly, "Transgender teens speak," https://ursamajornews.com/756/opinion/transgender-teens-speak/ (accessed 22 April 2018).

11. Anna Tetlow, Forces.net, "Does Trump Know Transgender Soldiers Served In The Civil War?" https://www.forces.net/news/does-trump-know-transgender-soldiers-served-civil-war (accessed 22 April 2018).

12. Trans Media Watch, "A Trans Timeline," http://www.transmediawatch.org/timeline.html (accessed 22 April 2018).

13. Ibid.

14. Ibid.

15. Ibid.

16. The Washington Post, "Hate in America is on the Rise," https://www.washingtonpost.com/opinions/hate-in-america-is-on-the-rise/2017/11/25/33808364-c94d-11e7-8321-481fd63f174d_story.html?utm_term=.f6f38491181f (accessed 22 April 2018).

17. Ryan Anderson and Roger Severino, The Heritage Foundation, "Proposed Obamacare Gender Identity Mandate Threatens Freedom of Conscience and the Independence of Physicians," https://www.heritage.org/health-care-reform/report/proposed-obamacare-

gender-identity-mandate-threatens-freedom-conscience (accessed 22 April 2018).

18. Emma Green.The Atlantic, "The Man Behind Trump's Religious-Freedom Agenda for Health Care," https://www.theatlantic.com/politics/archive/2017/06/the-man-behind-trumps-religious-freedom-agenda-for-health-care/528912/ (accessed 22 April 2018).

19. Emmarie Huetteman, Kaiser Health News, "At New Health Office, 'Civil Rights' Means Doctors' Right To Say No To Patients," https://khn.org/news/at-new-health-office-civil-rights-means-doctors-right-to-say-no-to-patients/ (accessed 22 April 2018).

20. Ibid

21. Eric Teetsel, The Kansas City Star, "The Kansas Republican Party is taking a stance on transgender identity," http://www.kansascity.com/opinion/readers-opinion/guest-commentary/article205581414.html (accessed 22 April 2018).

22. Dale O'Leary and Peter Sprigg, Family Research Council, "Understanding and Responding to the Transgender Movement," https://www.frc.org/transgender (accessed 22 April 2018).

23. SPLC, "Family Research Council," https://www.splcenter.org/fighting-hate/extremist-files/group/family-research-council (accessed 22 April 2018).

24. Brynn Tannehill, Huffpost, "And Then They Came for Transgender People," https://www.huffingtonpost.com/brynn-tannehill/and-then-they-came-for-tr_b_9258678.html (accessed 22 April 2018).

CHAPTER 1: OUR ANTI-TRANSGENDER MOMENT

1. Virginia's Legislative Information System, "House Bill 1612," https://lis.virginia.gov/cgi-bin/legp604.exe?171+ful+HB1612 (accessed 22 April 2018).

2. This is seen in many places, including: https://www.theodysseyonline.com/could-we-all-just-piss-in-peace (accessed 7 April 2018).

https://accidentallygay.com/2017/01/08/more-work-stuff/ (accessed 7 May 2018).
https://kathys-comments.com/2018/bathroom-bill-meme (accessed 7 May 2018).
And many others

3. Mitch Kellaway, Advocate, "Trans Folks Respond to 'Bathroom Bills' With #WeJustNeedtoPee Selfies," https://www.advocate.com/politics/transgender/2015/03/14/trans-folks-respond-bathroom-bills-wejustneedtopee-selfies (accessed 7 May 2018).

4. Lexie Cannes State Of Trans, "Cis woman, accused of being a "boy," was manhandled and kicked out of a women's bathroom; sues," https://lexiecannes.com/2015/06/15/cis-woman-accused-of-being-a-boy-was-manhandled-and-kicked-out-of-a-womens-bathroom-sues/ (accessed 22 April 2018).

5. Dee Culp, NEPA Scene, "LIVING YOUR TRUTH: Restroom incident at Kildare's brings up gender identity issues in Scranton," http://nepascene.com/2015/08/living-your-truth-restroom-incident-kildares-brings-up-gender-identity-issues-scranton/ (accessed 22 April 2018).

6. Eric Nicholson, Dallas Observer, "Self-Appointed Bathroom Cop Catches Dallas Woman Using Women's Restroom," http://www.dallasobserver.com/news/self-appointed-bathroom-cop-catches-dallas-woman-using-womens-restroom-8259104 (accessed 22 April 2018).

7. David Ferguson, Raw Story, "Kentucky woman says man beat her for looking too masculine — as people stood by and watched," https://www.rawstory.com/2016/05/kentucky-woman-says-man-beat-her-for-looking-too-masculine-as-people-stood-by-and-watched/#.VzeHprEcnM8.facebook (accessed 22 April 2018).

8. Matt DeRienzo, News Times, "Woman mistaken for transgender harassed in Walmart bathroom," https://www.newstimes.com/local/article/Woman-mistaken-for-transgender-harassed-in-7471666.php#photo-10075102 (accessed 22 April 2018).

9. Lexie Cannes State Of Trans, "Arrested cis woman fails vagina inspection, jailed with 40 men in common cell; files

$ 5 million lawsuit," https://lexiecannes.com/2016/09/18/arrested-cis-woman-fails-vagina-inspection-jailed-with-40-men-in-common-cell/ (accessed 22 April 2018).

10. Talking Points Memo, "Fox Host: 'Bathroom Bills' Are A 'Solution In Search Of A Problem'," https://talking pointsmemo.com/livewire/chris-wallace-bathroom-bills (accessed 22 April 2018).

11. Agnes Gereben Schaefer, The RAND Blog, "On RAND's Research Findings Regarding Transgender Military Personnel Policy," https://www.rand.org/blog/2018/03/on-rands-research-findings-regarding-transgender-military.html (accessed 22 April 2018).

12. Agnes Gereben Schaefer, RAND, "Impact of Transgender Personnel on Readiness and Health Care Costs in the U.S. Military Likely to Be Small," https://www.rand.org/news/press/2016/06/30.html (accessed 22 April 2018).

13. RealDonaldTrump, 26 July 2017, "After consultation with my Generals..." https://twitter.com/realDonaldTrump/status/890193981585444864?ref_src=twsrc%5Etfw&ref_url=https%3A%2F%2Fwww.cnn.com%2F2017%2F07%2F26%2Fpolitics%2Ftrump-military-transgender%2Findex.html (accessed 22 April 2018).

14. Mark Joseph Stern, Slate, "Trump's Trans Troops Ban Will Never Take Effect," https://slate.com/news-and-politics/2018/03/trumps-new-trans-troops-ban-is-still-unconstitutional.html (accessed 22 April 2018).

15. SPLC, "Family Research Council," https://www.splcenter.org/fighting-hate/extremist-files/group/family-research-council (accessed 22 April 2018).

16. Lambda Legal, "Exhibit 2: Department of Defense Report and Recommendations on Military Service by Transgender Persons (Feb. 2018)," https://www.lambdalegal.org/sites/default/files/legal-docs/downloads/dkt._216-2._dod_report_and_recommendations_feb_2018 1.pdf (accessed 22 April 2018).

17. Ellen Mitchell, The Hill, "Dems want Mattis to reveal experts behind Pentagon transgender policy," http://thehill.com/policy/defense/382853-dems-want-

mattis-to-reveal-experts-behind-pentagon-transgender-policy (accessed 22 April 2018).

CHAPTER 2: WHAT THE ACTIVISTS BABBLE

1. Zack Ford, ThinkProgress, "How The Incendiary Rhetoric Against Transgender Youth Is Escalating," https://thinkprogress.org/how-the-incendiary-rhetoric-against-transgender-youth-is-escalating-c315a6901beb/ (accessed 22 April 2018).
2. Alan Cooperman, Washington Post, "Navy Chaplain Guilty Of Disobeying an Order," http://www.washington post.com/wp-dyn/content/article/2006/09/14/AR20060 91401544.html (accessed 22 April 2018).
3. SPLC, "American Family Association," https://www.splc enter.org/fighting-hate/extremist-files/group/american-family-association (accessed 22 April 2018).
4. GLAAD, "Scott Lively," https://www.glaad.org/cap /scott-lively (accessed 22 April 2018).
5. GLAAD, "Keith Ablow," https://www.glaad.org/cap /keith-ablow (accessed 22 April 2018).
6. Ibid.
7. Michael W. Chapman, CNS News, "Johns Hopkins Psychiatrist: Transgender is 'Mental Disorder;' Sex Change 'Biologically Impossible'," https://www.cnsnews.com/ news/article/michael-w-chapman/johns-hopkins-psychiatrist-transgender-mental-disorder-sex-change (accessed 22 April 2018).
8. Gavin McInnes, Thought Catalog, "Transphobia Is Perfectly Natural," https://thoughtcatalog.com/gavin-mcinnes/ 2014/08/ transphobia-is-perfectly-natural/(accessed 9 April 2018).
9. SPLC, "American College of Pediatricians," https://www.splcenter.org/fighting-hate/extremist-files/group/american-college-pediatricians (accessed 22 April 2018).
10. The New Atlantis, "Sexuality and Gender: Frequently Asked Questions,"

https://www.thenewatlantis.com/publications/frequently-asked-questions-sexuality-and-gender   Reported   in question 17. (accessed 22 April 2018).

11. Lawrence S. Mayer, and Paul R. McHugh The New Atlantis, "Special Report: Sexuality and Gender," https://www.thenewatlantis.com/docLib/20160819_TNA 50SexualityandGender.pdf (accessed 22 April 2018).

12. ACPeds, "Gender Ideology Harms Children," https://www.acpeds.org/the-college-speaks/position-statements/gender-ideology-harms-children (accessed 22 April 2018).

13. Paul R. McHugh, First Things, "Surgical Sex," https://www.firstthings.com/article/2004/11/surgical-sex (accessed 22 April 2018).

14. First Things, "February Letters: 70," https://www.first things.com/article/2005/02/science-and-climate-change (accessed 22 April 2018).

15. Public Discourse, "Author Archives: Walt Heyer," http://www.thepublicdiscourse.com/author/walt-heyer/ (accessed 22 April 2018).

16. The Daily Signal, "Walt Heyer," https://www.daily signal.com/author/walt-heyer/ (accessed 22 April 2018).

17. David Cary Hart, The Slowly Boiled Frog, "'Billy' - Recycling anti-gay to anti-trans,' http://www.slowlyboiledfrog .com/2018/03/billy-recycling-anti-gay-to-anti-trans.html (accessed 23 April 2018).

18. SPLC, "Alliance Defending Freedom developed a stable of anti-LGBT 'expert' witnesses," https://www.splcenter .org/hatewatch/2017/12/13/alliance-defending-freedom-developed-stable-anti-lgbt-expert-witnesses (accessed 23 April 2018).

19. SPLC, "Alliance Defending Freedom," https://www. splcenter.org/fighting-hate/extremist-files/group/ alliance-defending-freedom (accessed 23 April 2018).

20. SPLC, "Alliance Defending Freedom developed a stable of anti-LGBT 'expert' witnesses," https://www.splcenter .org/hatewatch/2017/12/13/alliance-defending-freedom-developed-stable-anti-lgbt-expert-witnesses (accessed 23 April 2018).

21. ACPeds, "About Us," https://www.acpeds.org/about-us (accessed 23 April 2018).
22. Society for Adolescent Health and Medicine, "SAHM Responds to Dr. Michelle Cretella," https://www.ado lescenthealth.org/SAHM-News/SAHM-Responds-to-Dr-Michelle-Cretella.aspx (accessed 23 April 2018).
23. Ibid.
24. Samantha Allen, Daily Beast, "Anti-LGBT Doc Paul McHugh: I Will Not Be Silenced," https://www.thedailybeast.com/anti-lgbt-doc-paul-mchugh-i-will-not-be-silenced (accessed 23 April 2018).
25. Zack Ford, ThinkProgress, "The Truth About The Massive New Study That Has Captivated Anti-LGBT Groups," https://thinkprogress.org/about-that-not-born-this-way-study-b3e07d0354f5/ (accessed 23 April 2018).
26. The Baltimore Sun, "Hopkins faculty disavow 'troubling' report on gender and sexuality," http://www.baltimore sun.com/news/opinion/oped/bs-ed-lgbtq-hopkins-20160928-story.html (accessed 23 April 2018).
27. Chris Beyrer, Robert W. Blum, and Tonia C. Poteat, Daily Beast, "Anti-LGBT Doc Paul McHugh: I Will Not Be Silenced," https://www.thedailybeast.com/anti-lgbt-doc-paul-mchugh-i-will-not-be-silenced (accessed 23 April 2018).
28. VUMC, "To Whom It May Concern," https://www.vumc.org/lgbti/files/lgbti/publication_files/ExpertLGBTIConcensusLetter.pdf (accessed 23 April 2018).
29. Rhodes Perry, Trans Equality Now, "Fight Back and Help Defeat Anti-Transgender State Legislation!" https://medium.com/transequalitynow/fight-back-and-help-defeat-anti-transgender-state-legislation-25f75437 a955 (accessed 23 April 2018).
30. Ibid.
31. Heather Hogan, Autostraddle, "Persecuting Trans Women: Finally a Thing Breitbart and The Religious Right Can Agree On," https://www.autostraddle.com/persecuting-trans-people-finally-a-thing-breitbart-and-the-religious-right-can-agree-on-370270/ (accessed 23 April 2018).

32. Jason Wilson, The Guardian, "'Biology is not bigotry': conservative writers react to ban on trans troops," https://www.theguardian.com/us-news/2017/jul/28/ conservative-writers-trump-transgender-troops-ban- military-writing (accessed 23 April 2018).
33. Rachael Bade and Josh Dawsey, Politico, "Inside Trump's snap decision to ban transgender troops," https://www.politico.com/story/2017/07/26/trump- transgender-military-ban-behind-the-scenes-240990 (accessed 23 April 2018).
34. Jonathan Shorman and Hunter Woodall, The Wichita Eagle, "Kansas GOP votes to 'oppose all efforts to validate transgender identity'," http://www.kansas.com/ news/politics-government/article200798114.html (accessed 23 April 2018).
35. Ryan T. Anderson, The Heritage Foundations, "A New York Times Writer's Reckless Hit Piece on My Transgender Book," https://www.heritage.org/gender/commentary/ new-york-times-writers-reckless-hit-piece-my- transgender-book (accessed 23 April 2018).
36. Amelia Gapin, "No, misgendering me is not okay or justifiable. Yes, this is a big deal." http://www.amelia. run/2014/01/02/misgendering-okay-justifiable-yes-big- deal/ (accessed 23 April 2018).
37. ACPeds, "In the Media," in the April 19 2016 link. https://www.acpeds.org/the-college-speaks/in-the-media (accessed 23 April 2018).
38. SPLC, "Family Research Council," https://www .splcenter.org/fighting-hate/extremist-files/group/ family-research-council (accessed 22 April 2018).
39. Cathy Ruse, Family Research Council, "Public School Assembly Tells Kids That Sex Changes Are Perfectly Normal," https://www.frc.org/op-eds/public-school- assembly-tells-kids-that-sex-changes-are-perfectly-normal (accessed 23 April 2018).
40. Brynn Tannehill, Huffpost, "10 Things Transphobes Say That Make Me *Facepalm*," https://www.huff ingtonpost.com/brynn-tannehill/transphobes_b_3780432 .html (accessed 23 April 2018).

CHAPTER 3: TRANSITIONERS TELL THEIR STORIES

1. Public Discourse, "Author Archives: Walt Heyer," http://www.thepublicdiscourse.com/author/walt-heyer/ (accessed 23 April 2018). This page lists numerous anti-transarticles by Heyer.

2. Zack Ford, ThinkProgress, "'I was enraged to see my story distorted and used': Detransitioners object to anti-transgender book: The Heritage Foundation's Ryan T. Anderson never reached out to these detransitioners." https://thinkprogress.org/detransitioner-ryan-anderson-transgender-25fad9803c2e/ (accessed 23 April 2018).

3. Ibid.

4. Ibid.

5. Ibid.

6. Kenneth J. Zucker, Susan J. Bradley, "Gender Identity Disorder and Psychosexual Problems in Children and Adolescents,"https://books.google.com/books/about/Gender_Identity_Disorder_and_Psychosexua.html?id=atfTHGjjVeIC (accessed 23 April 2018).

7. Zinnia Jones, Gender Analysis, "When 'desisters' aren't: De-desistance in childhood and adolescent gender dysphoria," https://genderanalysis.net/2017/10/when-desisters-arent-de-desistance-in-childhood-and-adolescent-gender-dysphoria/ (accessed 23 April 2018).

8. Erin Anderssen, The Globe and Mail, "Gender identity debate swirls over CAMH psychologist, transgender program," https://beta.theglobeandmail.com/news/toronto/gender-identity-debate-swirls-over-camh-psychologist-transgender-program/article28758828/?ref=http://www.theglobeandmail.com& (accessed 23 April 2018).

9. Thomas D. Steensma and Peggy T. Cohen-Kettenis, Journal of the American Academy of Child & Adolescent Psychiatry, "More Than Two Developmental Pathways in Children With Gender Dysphoria?" http://www.jaacap.com/article/S0890-8567(14)00801-6/fulltext (accessed 23 April 2018).

10. Zinnia Jones, Gender Analysis, "When 'desisters' aren't: De-desistance in childhood and adolescent gender dysphoria," https://genderanalysis.net/2017/10/when-desisters-arent-de-desistance-in-childhood-and-adolescent-gender-dysphoria/ (accessed 23 April 2018).

11. Zack Ford, ThinkProgress, "The pernicious junk science stalking trans kids: The 'desistance' myth doesn't explain why transgender children are thriving." https://thinkprogress.org/transgender-children-desist ance-a5caf61fc5c6/ (accessed 23 April 2018).

12. Jennifer Finney Boylan, Amazon.com, "She's Not There: A Life in Two Genders," https://www.amazon.com/Shes-Not-There-Life-Genders/dp/0385346972/ (accessed 23 April 2018).

13. Jamison Green, Amazon.com, "Becoming a Visible Man," https://www.amazon.com/Becoming-Visible-Man-Jami son-Green/dp/082651457X (accessed 23 April 2018).

14. Daphne Scholinski, Amazon.com, "The Last Time I Wore A Dress," https://www.amazon.com/Last-Time-Wore-Dress/dp/1573226963/ (accessed 23 April 2018).

15. Donna Rose, Amazon.com. "Wrapped In Blue: A Journey of Discovery," https://www.amazon.com/Wrapped-Blue-Discovery-Donna-Rose/dp/0972955305/ (accessed 23 April 2018).

16. Samantha Adams, Barnes and Noble, "Through the Jungle: A Traveler's Guide," https://www.barnesandnoble.com/w/through-the-jungle-samantha-w-adams/1114225372 (accessed 23 April 2018).

CHAPTER 4: WHAT MAKES US HARRY OR SALLY?

1. National Institute of Health, "How many people are affected by or at risk for Klinefelter syndrome (KS)?" https://www.nichd.nih.gov/health/topics/klinefelter/cond itioninfo/risk (accessed 23 April 2018).

2. Ibid.

3. Genetics Home Reference, "Turner syndrome," https://ghr.nlm.nih.gov/condition/turner-syndrome# statistics (accessed 23 April 2018).

4. Ibid.

5. Genetics Home Reference, "Swyer syndrome," https://ghr.nlm.nih.gov/condition/swyer-syndrome# (accessed 23 April 2018).

6. A de la Chapelle, NCBI, "Analytic review: nature and origin of males with XX sex chromosomes." https://www.ncbi.nlm.nih.gov/pmc/articles/PMC1762158 / (accessed 23 April 2018).

7. Anthony F. Bogaert, "Asexuality: Prevalence and Associated Factors in a National Probability Sample," https://www.jstor.org/stable/4423785?seq=1#page_scan_tab_contents (accessed 23 April 2018).

8. Jody L. Herman, et al., The Williams Institute, "Age of Individuals Who Identify As Transgender In the United States," https://williamsinstitute.law.ucla.edu/wp-content/uploads/TransAgeReport.pdf (accessed 23 April 2018).

9. Brenda K. Todd, et al., Infant and Child Development, Wiley Online Library, "Sex differences in children's toy preferences: A systematic review, meta-regression, and meta-analysis," https://onlinelibrary.wiley.com/doi/abs/10.1002/icd.2064 (accessed 23 April 2018).

10. Janice M. Hassett, et al., NCBI, "Sex differences in rhesus monkey toy preferences parallel those of children," https://www.ncbi.nlm.nih.gov/pmc/articles/PMC2583786 / (accessed 23 April 2018).

11. Gerianne M Alexander and Melissa Hines, Evolution and Human Behavior, "Sex differences in response to children's toys in nonhuman primates (*Cercopithecus aethiops sabaeus*)," http://www.ehbonline.org/article/S1090-5138 (02)00107-1/fulltext (accessed 23 April 2018).

12. Colapinto, John. 2000. *As nature made him: the boy who was raised as a girl*. Toronto: HarperCollins Publishers.

13. New England Journal of Medicine, "Discordant Sexual Identity in Some Genetic Males with Cloacal Exstrophy Assigned to Female Sex at Birth," http://www.nejm.

org/doi/full/10.1056/NEJMoa022236 (accessed 23 April 2018).

14. Ai-Min Baoa and Dick F. Swaab, Science Direct, "Sexual differentiation of the human brain: Relation to gender identity, sexual orientation and neuropsychiatric disorders," https://www.sciencedirect.com/science/article/pii/S0091302211000252?via%3Dihub (accessed 23 April 2018).

15. M. Leinung and C. Wu, NCBI, "The Biologic Basis of Transgender Identity: 2D:4D Finger Length Ratios Implicate a Role For Prenatal Androgen Activity." https://www.ncbi.nlm.nih.gov/pubmed/28332875 (accessed 23 April 2018).

16. S. Vujović, et al., NCBI, "Finger length ratios in Serbian transsexuals." https://www.ncbi.nlm.nih.gov/pubmed/24982993 (accessed 23 April 2018).

17. M. S. Wallien, et al., NCBI, "2D:4D finger-length ratios in children and adults with gender identity disorder." https://www.ncbi.nlm.nih.gov/pubmed/18585715 (accessed 23 April 2018).

18. Lauren Hare, et al., Biological Psychiatry, "Androgen Receptor Repeat Length Polymorphism Associated with Male-to-Female Transsexualism,"http://www.biologicalpsychiatryjournal.com/article/S0006-3223(08)01087-1/fulltext (accessed 23 April 2018).

19. Oliver Moody, The Times, "Science pinpoints DNA behind gender identity," https://www.thetimes.co.uk/article/science-pinpoints-dna-behind-gender-identity-3vmrgrdnv (accessed 23 April 2018).

20. Jeff Taylor, LGBTQ Nation, "Scientists discover DNA that could be responsible for gender identity," https://www.lgbtqnation.com/2018/03/scientists-discover-dna-responsible-gender-identity/ (accessed 23 April 2018).

21. Eva-Katrin Bentz, et al., Fertility and Sterility, "A polymorphism of the CYP17 gene related to sex steroid metabolism is associated with female-to-male but not male-to-female transsexualism," http://www.fertstert.org/

article/S0015-0282(07)01228-9/fulltext (accessed 23 April 2018).

22. Stephen M. Rosenthal, The Journal of Clinical Endocrinology & Metabolism, "Approach to the Patient: Transgender Youth: Endocrine Considerations," https://academic.oup.com/jcem/article/99/12/4379/2833 862 (accessed 23 April 2018).

23. J. Cortés-Cortés, et al., NCBI, "Genotypes and Haplotypes of the Estrogen Receptor α Gene (ESR1) Are Associated With Female-to-Male Gender Dysphoria." https://www.ncbi.nlm.nih.gov/pubmed/28117266?dopt=Abstract (accessed 23 April 2018).

24. R. Fernández, et al., NCBI, "The (CA)n polymorphism of ERβ gene is associated with FtM transsexualism." https://www.ncbi.nlm.nih.gov/ pubmed/24274329?dopt=Abstract (accessed 23 April 2018).

25. Fu Yang, et al., Nature.com, "Genomic Characteristics of Gender Dysphoria Patients and Identification of Rare Mutations in RYR3 Gene,"https://www.nature.com/ articles/s41598-017-08655-x (accessed 23 April 2018).

26. F. L. Coolidge, et al., NCBI, "The heritability of gender identity disorder in a child and adolescent twin sample." https://www.ncbi.nlm.nih.gov/pubmed/12211624 (accessed 23 April 2018).

27. Milton Diamond, University of Hawaii, "Transsexuality Among Twins: Identity Concordance, Transition, Rearing, and Orientation," http://www.hawaii.edu/PCSS/biblio/ articles/2010to2014/2013-transsexuality.html (accessed 23 April 2018).

28. National Cancer Institute, "Diethylstilbestrol (DES) and Cancer," https://www.cancer.gov/about-cancer/causes-prevention/risk/hormones/des-fact-sheet (accessed 23 April 2018).

29. DES Daughter, DiEthylStilbestrol.co.uk, "Prenatal DiEthylStilbestrol Exposure in Males and Gender-related Disorders,"https://diethylstilbestrol.co.uk/prenatal-diethylstilbestrol-exposure-in-males-and-gender-related-disorders/ (accessed 24 April 2018).

30. National Institute of Health, "Endocrine Disruptors," https://www.niehs.nih.gov/health/topics/agents/endocrin e/index.cfm (accessed 24 April 2018).

31. Ibid.

32. Zana Percy, Environmental Health Journal, "Gestational exposure to phthalates and gender-related play behaviors in 8-year-old children: an observational study," https://ehjournal.biomedcentral.com/articles/10.1186/s12 940-016-0171-7 (accessed 24 April 2018).

33. Ruben C. Gur, Journal of Neuroscience, "Sex Differences in Brain Gray and White Matter in Healthy Young Adults: Correlations with Cognitive Performance," http://www.jneurosci.org/content/19/10/4065 (accessed 24 April 2018).

34. Eileen Luders, et al., NCBI, "Regional gray matter variation in male-to-female transsexualism," https://www.ncbi. nlm.nih.gov/pmc/articles/PMC2754583/ (accessed 24 April 2018).

35. GiuseppinaRametti, et al., Science Direct, "White matter microstructure in female to male transsexuals before cross-sex hormonal treatment. A diffusion tensor imaging study," https://www.sciencedirect.com/science/article/pii/S0022 395610001585#sec2.1 (accessed 24 April 2018).

36. J.-N. Zhou, et al., International Journal of Transgenderism, "A Sex Difference in the Human Brain and its Relation to Transsexuality,"http://faculty.bennington.edu/~sherman/ sex/TRANSGENDER.pdf (accessed 24 April 2018).The report is archived by Bennington.

37. F. P, Kruijver Journal of Clinical Endocrinology, PubMed, "Male-to-female transsexuals have female neuron numbers in a limbic nucleus." https://www.ncbi.nlm.nih. gov/m/pubmed/10843193/ (accessed 24 April 2018).

38. Jamison Green, Amazon.com, "Becoming a Visible Man," https://www.amazon.com/Becoming-Visible-Man-Jami son-Green/dp/082651457X (accessed 24 April 2018).

CHAPTER 5: GENDER IDENTITY AND AFFIRMATION
SURGERY

1. The Williams Institute, "Suicide Attempts among
   Transgender and Gender Non-Conforming Adults Findings
   of the National Transgender Discrimination Survey,"
   https://williamsinstitute.law.ucla.edu/wp-content/up
   loads/AFSP-Williams-Suicide-Report-Final.pdf (accessed
   24 April 2018).
2. WPATH, Standards of Care Version 7,"
   https://www.wpath.org/publications/soc (accessed 24
   April 2018).
3. Stated on the dust cover.
4. Zack Ford, ThinkProgress, "'I was enraged to see my story
   distorted and used': Detransitioners object to anti-
   transgender book. The Heritage Foundation's Ryan T.
   Anderson never reached out to these detransitioners."
   https://thinkprogress.org/detransitioner-ryan-anderson-
   transgender-25fad
   9803c2e/ (accessed 24 April 2018).
5. Griet De Cuypere, et al., ResearchGate, "Long-term follow-
   up: Psychosocial outcome of Belgian transsexuals after sex
   reassignment surgery," https://www.researchgate.net/
   publication/247335377_Long-term_follow-up_Psycho
   social_outcome_of_Belgian_transsexuals_after_sex_reas
   signment_surgery (accessed 24 April 2018).
6. Ulrike Ruppin and Friedemann Pfäfflin, Archives of Sexual
   Behavior, Springer Link, "Long-Term Follow-Up of Adults
   with Gender Identity Disorder," https://link.springer.com
   /article/10.1007/s10508-014-0453-5 (accessed 24 April
   2018).
7. European Association of Urology, "First accurate data
   showing male to female transgender surgery can give better
   life," https://www.eurekalert.org/pub_releases/2018-03/
   eaou-fad031518.php (accessed 24 April 2018).
8. Cecilia Dhejne, et al., PLOS ONE, "Long-Term Follow-Up of
   Transsexual Persons Undergoing Sex Reassignment
   Surgery: Cohort Study in Sweden,"

http://journals.plos.org/plosone/article?id=10.1371/journ
al.pone.0016885 (accessed 24 April 2018).

9. TransAdvocate, "Fact check: study shows transition makes trans people suicidal," http://transadvocate.com /fact-check-study-shows-transition-makes-trans-people-suicidal_n_15483.htm (accessed 24 April 2018).

10. G Heylens, et al., NCBI, "Effects of different steps in gender reassignment therapy on psychopathology: a prospective study of persons with a gender identity disorder." https://www.ncbi.nlm.nih.gov/pubmed/24344788 (accessed 24 April 2018).

11. Annika Johansson, et al., Springer Link, "A Five-Year Follow-Up Study of Swedish Adults with Gender Identity Disorder," https://link.springer.com/article/10.1007%2Fs 10508-009-9551-1 (accessed 24 April 2018). Originally in *Archives of Sexual Behavior.*

12. Mohammad Hassan Murad, et al., Mayo Clinic, "Hormonal therapy and sex reassignment: A systematic review and meta-analysis of quality of life and psychosocial outcomes," https://mayoclinic.pure.elsevier.com/en/publications/hor monal-therapy-and-sex-reassignment-a-systematic-review-and-met (accessed 24 April 2018).

13. Nataša Jokić-Begić, et al., The Scientific World Journal, "Psychosocial Adjustment to Sex Reassignment Surgery: A Qualitative Examination and Personal Experiences of Six Transsexual Persons in Croatia," https://www.hindawi .com/journals/tswj/2014/960745/ (accessed 24 April 2018).

14. Ulrike Ruppin and Friedemann Pfäfflin, Springer Link, "Long-Term Follow-Up of Adults with Gender Identity Disorder," https://link.springer.com/article/10.1007/ s10508-014-0453-5 (accessed 24 April 2018). Originally in *Archives of Sexual Behavior.*

15. Steven Weyers, et al., ResearchGate, "Long-term Assessment of the Physical, Mental, and Sexual Health among Transsexual Women," https://www.researchgate .net/publication/23553588_Long-term_Assessment_of_ the_Physical_Mental_and_Sexual_Health_among_Trans

sexual_Women (accessed 24 April 2018). Originally in *Journal of Sexual Medicine.*

16. U. Ruppin and F. Pfäfflin, Springer Link, "Long-Term Follow-Up of Adults with Gender Identity Disorder," https://link.springer.com/article/10.1007/s10508-014-0453-5 (accessed 24 April 2018). Originally in *Journal of Sexual Behavior.*

17. Cecilia Dhejne, et al., Springer Link, "An Analysis of All Applications for Sex Reassignment Surgery in Sweden, 1960–2010: Prevalence, Incidence, and Regrets," https://link.springer.com/article/10.1007/s10508-014-0300-8 (accessed 24 April 2018). Originally in *Journal of Sexual Behavior.*

18. U. Ruppin and F. Pfäfflin, Springer Link, "Long-Term Follow-Up of Adults with Gender Identity Disorder," https://link.springer.com/article/10.1007/s10508-014-0453-5 (accessed 24 April 2018). Originally in *Journal of Sexual Behavior.*

19. B. Ozata, et al., European Psychiatry, "EPA-0185 - Effects of sex reassignment surgery on quality of life and mental health in transsexuals," http://www.europsy-journal.com/article/S0924-9338(14)77643-6/abstract (accessed 24 April 2018).

20. Cornell University, "What does the scholarly research say about the effect of gender transition on transgender well-being?" https://whatweknow.inequality.cornell.edu/topics/lgbt-equality/what-does-the-scholarly-research-say-about-the-well-being-of-transgender-people/ (accessed 24 April 2018).

21. Nathaniel Frank, Endocrine Today, "Gender transition positively affects well-being of transgender adults," https://www.healio.com/endocrinology/news/online/%7B3164b688-041b-444e-89c0-82e3c5a508e3%7D/gender-transition-positively-affects-well-being-of-transgender-adults (accessed 24 April 2018).

22. Stated on the dust cover.

23. WPATH, "Position Statement on Medical Necessity of Treatment, Sex Reassignment, and Insurance Coverage in

the U.S.A.," https://www.wpath.org/newsroom/medical-necessity-statement (accessed 24 April 2018).

CHAPTER 6: CHILDHOOD DYSPHORIA AND PERSISTENCE

1. Based upon my personal discussions with hundreds of transitioned transgender patients. Ryan T. Anderson, to the best of my knowledge, has never knowingly spoken to a transitioned patient in his life.
2. Petula Dvorak, The Washington Post, "Transgender at Five," https://www.washingtonpost.com/local/transgender-at-five/2012/05/19/gIQABfFkbU_story.html?utm_term=.0ec2a7a529d1 (accessed 28 March 2018).
3. Jesse Singal, The Cut, "How the Fight over Transgender Kids Got a Leading Sex Researcher Fired," https://www.thecut.com/2016/02/fight-over-trans-kids-got-a-researcher-fired.html (accessed 24 April 2018).
4. Ibid.
5. SPLC, "American College of Pediatricians," https://www.splcenter.org/fighting-hate/extremist-files/group/american-college-pediatricians (accessed 22 April 2018).
6. Richard Klaus, The Christian Post, "Transgender Ideas Never Stand Alone and Never Stand Still," https://www.christianpost.com/news/transgender-ideas-never-stand-alone-and-never-stand-still-222084/print.html (accessed 24 April 2018).
7. DSM Guide Wikia, "Gender Dysphoria," http://dsm.wikia.com/wiki/Gender_Dysphoria (accessed 24 April 2018).
8. Wylie C. Hembree, et al., The Journal of Clinical Endocrinology & Metabolism, "Endocrine Treatment of Transsexual Persons: An Endocrine Society Clinical Practice Guideline," http://www.cpath.ca/wp-content/uploads/2009/12/JCEM-20099493132-3154.pdf (accessed 24 April 2018).

9. Anderson's quote is from Zucker et al., "A Developmental, Biophysical Model for the Treatment of Children with Gender Identity Disorder."

10. Zack Ford, ThinkProgress, "The pernicious junk science stalking trans kids The 'desistance' myth doesn't explain why transgender children are thriving." https://thinkprogress.org/transgender-children-desistance-a5caf61fc5c6/ (accessed 24 April 2018).

11. HumanRights.Gov.Au, "Family Court of Australia Re: Kelvin [2017] FamCAFC 258," https://www.human rights.gov.au/sites/default/files/Re%2BKelvin%2B30%2B November%2B2017.pdf (accessed 24 April 2018).

12. Tomas D. Steensma, et al., Semantic Scholar, "Factors Associated with Desistence and Persistence of Childhood Gender Dysphoria: A Quantitative Follow-up Study," https://pdfs.semanticscholar.org/e2fb/c2935513f405712ec d752b2940deab020f8e.pdf (accessed 24 April 2018).

13. SPLC, "Anti-LGBT," https://www.splcenter.org/fighting-hate/extremist-files/ideology/anti-lgbt (accessed 24 April 2018).

14. Kenneth J. Zucker, et al., ResearchGate, "A Developmental, Biopsychosocial Model for the Treatment of Children with Gender Identity Disorder." https://www.researchgate.net/ publication/223135175_A_Developmental_Biopsychosoci al_Model_for_the_Treatment_of_Children_with_Gender _Identity_Disorder (accessed 24 April 2018).Originally in *Journal of Homosexuality*.

15. Alix Spiegel, NPR, "Two Families Grapple with Sons' Gender Identity," https://www.npr.org/2008/05/07/ 90247842/two-families-grapple-with-sons-gender-preferences (accessed 24 April 2018).

16. Bossip Staff, BOSSIP, "Family Blames Anti-Gay Therapist For The Suicide Of Their Son, Brother," https://bossip.com /395991/family-blames-anti-gay-therapist-for-the-suicide-of-their-son-brother-43081/ (accessed 24 April 2018).

17. Dawn Ennis, Los Angeles Blade, "Ohio trans boy seeks judge's OK to avoid conversion therapy," http://www.losangelesblade.com/2018/02/08/ohio-trans-

boy-seeks-judges-ok-avoid-conversion-therapy/ (accessed 24 April 2018).

18. Ryan T. Anderson, The Heritage Foundation, "Parents Just Lost Custody of Teenage Daughter Who Wants to 'Transition' to a Boy: What You Need to Know," https://www.heritage.org/gender/commentary/parents-just-lost-custody-teenage-daughter-who-wants-transition-boy-what-you-need (accessed 24 April 2018).

19. Carl Charles, The Advocate, "A Firsthand Account of the Torture of 'Conversion' Therapy," https://www.advocate.com/commentary/2015/11/02/firsthand-account-torture-conversion-therapy (accessed 24 April 2018).

20. The #BornPerfect campaign seeks to outlaw the practice of "reparative" or "conversion therapy" in every U.S. state by 2019. California, New Jersey, Washington, D.C., Oregon, and Illinois have already passed laws banning the use of these medically debunked counseling methods on minors, which have been denounced as ineffective and harmful by every major mental health and medical organization in the country. Because of the aggressive tactics and stigma central to these so-called therapies, many youth like me don't share their experiences with these horrific and unregulated attempts to "pray away the gay," or in my case, pray away the "trans," until much later in life.

21. Fallon Fox, Time, "Leelah Alcorn's Suicide: Conversion Therapy Is Child Abuse, http://time.com/3655718/leelah-alcorn-suicide-transgender-therapy/ (accessed 24 April 2018).

22. CatholicTrans, "Suicide note," https://catholictrans.wordpress.com/2015/01/03/leelah-alcorns-suicide-note-full-text/ (accessed 24 April 2018).

23. Zack Ford, ThinkProgress, "Study Suggests Anti-Trans Parents May Literally Be Killing Their Kids," https://thinkprogress.org/study-suggests-anti-trans-parents-may-literally-be-killing-their-kids-a2f06075c288/ (accessed 24 April 2018).

24. Samantha Allen, Daily Beast, "CALM DOWN: It's Absurd to Claim That Trans Kids Are Being 'Rushed' Into Transitioning: Ignore the alarmist commentators. Parents

of trans kids are not rushing their offspring through transitioning. The process is sensitively and carefully overseen," https://www.thedailybeast.com/its-absurd-to-claim-that-trans-kids-are-being-rushed-into-transitioning (accessed 24 April 2018).

25. Kristina R. Olson, et al., American Academy of Pediatrics, "Mental Health of Transgender Children Who Are Supported in Their Identities," http://pediatrics.aap publications.org/content/early/2016/02/24/peds.2015-3223 (accessed 24 April 2018).

26. A. L. de Vries, et al., NCBI, "Puberty suppression in adolescents with gender identity disorder: a prospective follow-up study." https://www.ncbi.nlm.nih.gov/pubmed/20646177 (accessed 24 April 2018).

27. The Endocrine Society, "San Diego clinic finds high need for treatment of transgender youth," https://www.eurek alert.org/pub_releases/2015-03/tes-sdc030615.php (accessed 24 April 2018).

28. Julia Serano, Medium, "Detransition, Desistance, and Disinformation: A Guide for Understanding Transgender Children Debates," https://medium.com/@juliaserano/detransition-desistance-and-disinformation-a-guide-for-understanding-transgender-children-993b7342946e (accessed 24 April 2018).

CHAPTER 7: GENDER AND NONCONFORMANCE

1. Jeanne Maglaty, Smithsonian.com, "When Did Girls Start Wearing Pink?: Every generation brings a new definition of masculinity and femininity that manifests itself in children's dress," https://www.smithsonianmag.com/arts-culture/when-did-girls-start-wearing-pink-1370097/ (accessed 27 April 2018).

2. Ibid.

3. Media Bias Fact Check, "Witherspoon Institute," https://mediabiasfactcheck.com/witherspoon-institute/ (accessed 27 April 2018).

4. Sofia Resnick, Salon, "Conservative group tries to sway SCOTUS on gay marriage with flawed study: New documents reveal the Witherspoon Institute recruited a university professor to try to manipulate public policy," https://www.salon.com/2013/03/11/conservative_group_tries_to_sway_scotus_on_gay_marriage_with_flawed_study_partner/ (accessed 27 April 2018).

5. Zack Ford, ThinkProgress, "Mark Regnerus Admits His 'Family Structures' Study Wasn't About Gay Parenting," https://thinkprogress.org/mark-regnerus-admits-his-family-structures-study-wasn-t-about-gay-parenting-554420fd83ea/ (accessed 27 April 2018).

6. Zack Ford, ThinkProgress, "Journal's Internal Audit Finds Flawed Gay Parenting Study To Be 'Bullshit'," https://thinkprogress.org/journals-internal-audit-finds-flawed-gay-parenting-study-to-be-bullshit-20b20ccf61f9/ (accessed 27 April 2018).

7. The Slowly Boiled Frog, "Witherspoon Institute reintroduces hate group CanaVox for about the fourth time," http://www.slowlyboiledfrog.com/2017/09/witherspoon-institute-reintroduces-hate.html (accessed 27 April 2018).

8. Henny M. W. Bos, et al., Family Process, "A Population-Based Comparison of Female and Male Same-Sex Parent and Different-Sex Parent Households," https://www.nllfs.org/images/uploads/bos-et-al-2017-family-process.pdf (accessed 27 April 2018).

9. Ellen C. Perrin, et al., American Academy of Pediatrics, "Promoting the Well-Being of Children Whose Parents Are Gay or Lesbian," http://pediatrics.aappublications.org/content/early/2013/03/18/peds.2013-0377 (accessed 27 April 2018).

10. Brief of *Amicus Curiae* American Sociological Association in Support of Respondent Kristin M. Perry And Respondent Edith Schlain Windsor, Supreme Court of the United States, http://www.asanet.org/sites/default/files/savvy/documents/ASA/pdfs/12-144_307_Amicus_%20(C_%20Gottlieb)_ASA_Same-Sex_Marriage.pdf (accessed 27 April 2018).

11. Wikipedia, "Bruno," https://en.wikipedia.org/wiki/Bruno_(2000_film) (accessed 27 April 2018).

12. R. J. Palacio, Amazon.com, "Wonder," https://www.ama zon.com/Wonder-R-J-Palacio/dp/0375869026/ (accessed 27 April 2018).
13. Wikipedia, "Free to Be... You and Me," https://en.wikipedia.org/wiki/Free_to_Be..._You_and_ Me (accessed 27 April 2018).
14. Ibid.
15. Wikipedia, "Rosey Grier," https://en.wikipedia.org /wiki/Rosey_Grier (accessed 27 April 2018).
16. Ibid
17. Trans Student Education Resources, "The Gender Unicorn," http://www.transstudent.org/gender (accessed 27 April 2018).

CHAPTER 8: POLICIES THAT DON'T SUCK

1. GLAD, "O'Donnabhain v. Commissioner of Internal Revenue: Victory," https://www.glad.org/cases/in-re-rhiannon-odonnabhain/ (accessed 27 April 2018).
2. Doug Mainwaring, LifeSiteNews, "Kansas Republicans vote to 'oppose all efforts to validate transgender identity'," https://www.lifesitenews.com/news/kansas-republicans-vote-to-oppose-all-efforts-to-validate-transgender-ident (accessed 27 April 2018).
3. EqualityKansas Facebook page, 18 February 2018, https://www.facebook.com/EqualityKansas/posts/203461 5203218846 (accessed 27 April 2018).
4. Hunter Woodall, The Kansas City Star, "Brownback's son-in-law defends Kansas GOP's stance on transgender identity," http://www.kansascity.com/news/local/news-columns-blogs/the-buzz/article203692529.html (accessed 27 April 2018).
5. Gregory H. Stanton, Genocide Watch, "The Ten Stages of Genocide by Dr. Gregory Stanton," http://genocide watch.org/genocide/tenstagesofgenocide.html (accessed 27 April 2018).
6. It was designed by Monica Helms in 1999 http://point5cc.com/the-history-of-the-transgender-flag/

(accessed 29 April 2018). It is featured on the cover of this book as the color theme.

7. SPLC, "Extremist Files: Groups,"https://www.splcenter.org/fighting-hate/extremist-files/groups (accessed 29 April 2018).

8. Brynn Tannehill, Huffpost, "And Then They Came for Transgender People," https://www.huffingtonpost.com/brynn-tannehill/and-then-they-came-for-tr_b_9258678.html (accessed 22 April 2018).

9. Eliza Gray, The New Republic, "Transitions," https://newrepublic.com/article/90519/transgender-civil-rights-gay-lesbian-lgbtq (accessed 29 April 2018).

10. Wikipedia, "List of unlawfully killed transgender people,"https://en.wikipedia.org/wiki/List_of_unlawfully_killed_transgender_people (accessed 29 April 2018).

11. Erin Fitzgerald, Media Matters, "A Comprehensive Guide to the Debunked "Bathroom Predator" Myth: Here's the Evidence Refuting the Myth about Trans-Inclusive Bathrooms," https://www.mediamatters.org/research/2016/05/05/comprehensive-guide-debunked-bathroom-predator-myth/210200 (accessed 29 April 2018).

12. Amanda Wicks, Complex.com, "More Republican legislators arrested for bathroom misconduct than trans people," http://www.complex.com/life/2016/03/republican-legislators-arrested-for-bathroom-misconduct (accessed 29 April 2018).

13. The Advocate, "New App Helps Find Safe Bathroom for LGBT Users," (accessed 29 April 2018). The meme also shows up in many other places, including Know Your Meme: http://knowyourmeme.com/photos/1109007-transgender-bathroom-debate.

14. Ryan Anderson and Melody Wood, The Heritage Foundation, "Gender Identity Policies in Schools: What Congress, the Courts, and the Trump Administration Should Do," https://www.heritage.org/education/report/gender-identity-policies-schools-what-congress-the-courts-and-the-trump (accessed 29 April 2018). Redrawn to match other charts in this chapter.

15. National Conference of State Legislatures, "'Bathroom Bill' Legislative Tracking," http://www.ncsl.org/research/ education/-bathroom-bill-legislative-tracking635951130. aspx (accessed 29 April 2018).

16. From Al Jazeera, "Trans man fights proposed bathroom ban with selfies," http://stream.aljazeera.com/story/2015 03121908-0024623. It featured "The New Choices" from a tweet by Cailin_Becoming. (accessed 29 April 2018).

17. Photo of Laurence Fishburne from Wikimedia Commons. https://commons.wikimedia.org/wiki/File:National_Mem orial_Day_Concert_2017_(34117818524)_(cropped).jpg (accessed 29 April 2018).

18. Stephanie Russell-Kraft, Religion and Politics, "The Clash between Religious Freedom and Equality Law," http://religionandpolitics.org/2017/03/28/the-clash- between-religious-freedom-and-equality-law/ (accessed 29 April 2018).

19. Ryan T. Anderson, The Heritage Foundation, "How to Think About Sexual Orientation and Gender Identity (SOGI) Policies and Religious Freedom," https://www.heritage .org/marriage-and-family/report/how-think-about-sexual- orientation-and-gender-identity-sogi-policies-and (accessed 29 April 2018).

20. Wikipedia, "LGBT-affirming religious groups," https:// en.wikipedia.org/wiki/LGBT-affirming_religious_ groups (accessed 29 April 2018).

21. APCI: "About Us," http://www.myapci.org/about.html (accessed 29 April 2018).

22. Sitemason.com, "The Alliance of Baptists Statement on Same Sex Marriage," http://www.sitemason.com /files/e10jfO/statementsamesexmarriage2004.pdf (accessed 29 April 2018).

23. The Church of England Education Office, "Valuing All God's Children: Guidance for Church of England schools on challenging homophobic, biphobic and transphobic bullying," https://www.churchofengland.org/sites/ default/files/2017-11/Valuing%20All%20God%27s%20 Children%27s%20Report_0.pdf (accessed 29 April 2018).

24. Unitarian Universalist Association, Home > Justice & Inclusion > LGBTQ Welcome & Equality. https://www. uua.org/lgbtq (accessed 29 April 2018).
25. Steve Sanders, Fortune, "Commentary: 'Religious Liberty' Is Not an Excuse to Deny Transgender People Medical Care," http://fortune.com/2018/01/18/transgender-health-medical-care-discrimination-religious-refused/ (accessed 29 April 2018).
26. Ryan T. Anderson, The Heritage Foundation, "How to Think About Discrimination: Race, Sex, and SOGI," https://www.heritage.org/gender/commentary/how-think-about-discrimination-race-sex-and-sogi-0 (accessed 29 April 2018).
27. AZFamily.com, "Transgender woman says she was denied service at Tempe bar," http://www.azfamily.com /story/29261562/transgender-woman-says-she-was-denied-service-at-tempe-bar (accessed 29 April 2018).
28. Matt Wood, Transgender Law Center, "California restaurant kicks out trans women, eats humble pie," https://transgenderlawcenter.org/archives/2713 (accessed 29 April 2018).
29. TCNE, "The Report of the 2015 U.S. Transgender Survey," https://transequality.org/sites/default/files/docs/usts/US TS-Full-Report-Dec17.pdf (accessed 29 April 2018).
30. Keren Landman, Vice.com, "Doctors Refuse to Treat Trans Patients More Often Than You Think," https://www.vice.com/en_us/article/j5vwgg/doctors-refuse-to-treat-trans-patients-more-often-than-you-think (accessed 29 April 2018).
31. The Williams Institute, "Suicide Attempts among Transgender and Gender Non-Conforming Adults: Findings of the National Transgender Discrimination Survey," https://williamsinstitute.law.ucla.edu/wp-content/up loads/AFSP-Williams-Suicide-Report-Final.pdf (accessed 29 April 2018).
32. Jaime M. Grant, et al., The Task Force, "National Transgender Discrimination Survey Report on health and health care," http://www.thetaskforce.org/static_html/

downloads/resources_and_tools/ntds_report_on_health.
pdf (accessed 29 April 2018).

33. Web.Archive.org, "Analysis: Tyra Hunter Wrongful Death
Trial," https://web.archive.org/web/20030418095928/
http://www.gpac.org/archive/news/notitle.html?cmd=vie
w&archive=news&msgnum=0050 (accessed 29 April
2018).

34. Ibid.

35. Khushbu Shah, Eater.com, "Indiana Passes Insane Law
Giving Restaurants the Right to Refuse Gay Diners,"
https://www.eater.com/2015/3/26/8296615/indiana-law-
religious-freedom-gay-lesbian-mike-pence (accessed 29
April 2018).

36. Ibid.

37. TCNE, "Tea Party Group Targets Trans Voters,"
https://transgenderequality.wordpress.com/2012/11/04/t
ea-party-group-targets-trans-voters/ (accessed 29 April
2018).

38. German Lopez, Vox.com, "States are making it a lot harder
for transgender people to vote,"
https://www.vox.com/identities/2016/10/25/13375146/tr
ansgender-voter-id-laws (accessed 29 April 2018).

39. The Williams Institue, "The Potential Impact of Voter
Identification Laws on Transgender Voters,"
http://williamsinstitute.law.ucla.edu/wp-content/upl
oads/Herman-Voter-ID-Apr-2012.pdf (accessed 29 April
2018).

40. Dom Phillips, The New York Times, "Torture and Killing of
Transgender Woman Stun Brazil," https://www.ny
times.com/2017/03/08/world/americas/brazil-trans
gender-killing-video.html (accessed 29 April 2018).

41. Avianne Tan, ABC News, "Trans Woman Found Beaten to
Death in Florida Believed to Be 10th Murder of Trans
Woman This Year," http://abcnews.go.com/US/trans-
woman-found-beaten-death-florida-believed-10th/story?
id=32638584 (accessed 29 April 2018).

42. John Paul Brammer, NBC News, "Prosecutors seek death
penalty in transgender teen's grisly killing: Investigators say
Missouri teen Ally Steinfeld was stabbed repeatedly in the

genitals, had her eyes gouged out and was set on fire." https://www.nbcnews.com/feature/nbc-out/prosecutors-seek-death-penalty-transgender-teen-s-grisly-murder-n862391 (accessed 29 April 2018).

43. Julia Serano, Medium, "Detransition, Desistance, and Disinformation: A Guide for Understanding Transgender Children Debates," https://medium.com/@juliaserano/detransition-desistance-and-disinformation-a-guide-for-understanding-transgender-children-993b7342946e (accessed 29 April 2018).

44. NCTE, "52 Things You Can Do for Transgender Equality," https://transequality.org/issues/resources/52-things-you-can-do-transgender-equality (accessed 29 April 2018).

CONCLUSION

1. SPLC, "Alliance Defending Freedom developed a stable of anti-LGBT 'expert' witnesses," https://www.splcenter.org/hatewatch/2017/12/13/alliance-defending-freedom-developed-stable-anti-lgbt-expert-witnesses (accessed 3 May 2018).

2. Tina Madison White, Amazon.com, "Deeply Flawed - No Matter What Your Views May Be," https://www.amazon.com/gp/review/RSHP62XQXIJYN (accessed 3 May 2018).

3. North Carolina General Assembly, "House Bill 2 / S.L. 2016-3: Public Facilities Privacy & Security Act." https://www.ncleg.net/gascripts/BillLookUp/BillLookUp.pl?Session=2015E2&BillID=HB2 (accessed 3 May 2018).

4. Wikipedia, "Public Facilities Privacy & Security Act," https://en.wikipedia.org/wiki/Public_Facilities_Privacy_%26_Security_Act (accessed 3 May 2018).

5. Ibid.

6. Andrew Sorensen, Time Warner Cable News, "HB2 Has Cost NC 1750 Jobs, $77 Million," https://web.archive.org/web/20161114234523/http://www.twcnews.com/nc/charlotte/news/2016/04/22/hb-2-has-cost-state-1750-jobs.html (accessed 3 May 2018).

7. Emery P. Dalesio, AP News, "AP Exclusive: Price tag of North Carolina's LGBT law: $3.76B," https://apnews.com/fa4528580f3e4a01bb68bcb272f1f0f8/ap-exclusive-bathroom-bill-cost-north-carolina-376b (accessed 3 May 2018).

8. LegiScan, "Bill Text: TX SB6," https://legiscan.com/TX/text/SB6/id/1445418 (accessed 3 May 2018).

9. Joshua Fechter, My San Antonio, "Study: Texas bathroom bill could cost state $3 billion in annual tourism business," https://www.mysanantonio.com/business/local/article/Study-Texas-bathroom-bill-could-cost-state-3-11078470.php (accessed 3 May 2018).

10. David Masci, Pew Research Center, "Key findings about Americans' views on religious liberty and nondiscrimination," http://www.pewresearch.org/fact-tank/2016/09/28/key-findings-about-americans-views-on-religious-liberty-and-nondiscrimination/ (accessed 3 May 2018).

11. Anna Brown, Pew Research Center, "Republicans, Democrats have starkly different views on transgender issues," http://www.pewresearch.org/fact-tank/2017/11/08/transgender-issues-divide-republicans-and-democrats/ (accessed 3 May 2018).

12. Wikipedia, "List of U.S. jurisdictions banning conversion therapy for minors," https://en.wikipedia.org/wiki/List_of_U.S._jurisdictions_banning_conversion_therapy_for_minors (accessed 3 May 2018).

13. Samantha Allen, Daily Beast, "LGBT 'Conversion Therapy' Is Dying a Quick Death Across America. Good." https://www.thedailybeast.com/lgbt-conversion-therapy-is-dying-a-quick-death-across-america-good (accessed 3 May 2018).

14. Zack Ford, ThinkProgress, "Johns Hopkins to resume gender-affirming surgeries after nearly 40 years," https://thinkprogress.org/johns-hopkins-transgender-surgery-5c9c428184c1/ (accessed 3 May 2018).

15. Mark Joseph Stern, Slate, "The Triumph of Transgender Rights in New Hampshire Is a GOP Rebuke to Mike Pence and Jeff Sessions," https://slate.com/human-interest/

2018/05/the-triumph-of-transgender-rights-in-new-hampshire-is-a-gop-rebuke-to-pence-and-sessions.html (accessed 5 May 2018).

16. The Trevor Project, "Trevor Lifeline," https://www.the trevorproject.org/ (accessed 3 May 2018).

AFTERWORD: THE CHALLENGE

1. Ryan T. Anderson, The Heritage Foundation, "A New York Times Writer's Reckless Hit Piece on My Transgender Book," https://www.heritage.org/gender/commentary/new-york-times-writers-reckless-hit-piece-my-transgender -book (accessed 22 April 2018).

2. Ryan T. Anderson, The Heritage Foundation, "Parents Just Lost Custody of Teenage Daughter Who Wants to 'Transition' to a Boy: What You Need to Know," https://www.heritage.org/gender/commentary/parents-just-lost-custody-teenage-daughter-who-wants-transition-boy-what-you-need (accessed 24 April 2018).

3. Trendsmap, "Ryan T. Anderson : 'Conversion'" therapy? That's the ...," https://www.trendsmap.com/twit ter/tweet/969713644014628864 (accessed 3 May 2018).

4. Michael Shermer, Scientific American, "What Is Pseudoscience?" https://www.scientificamerican.com/article/what-is-pseudoscience/ (accessed 3 May 2018).

5. Joe.My.God., "Hate Groups, Politics: Mutiny At The Anti-LGBT Heritage Foundation," http://www.joemygod .com/2017/04/28/mutiny-anti-lgbt-heritage-foundation/ (accessed 3 May 2018).

6. Ryan T. Anderson, The Heritage Foundation, "Sex Reassignment Doesn't Work. Here Is the Evidence." https://www.heritage.org/gender/commentary/sex-reas signment-doesnt-work-here-the-evidence (accessed 3 May 2018).

7. Griet De Cuypere, et al., ResearchGate, "Long-term follow-up: Psychosocial outcome of Belgian transsexuals after sex reassignment surgery,"https://www.researchgate.net/publication/247335377_Long-term_follow-up_Psychoso

cial_outcome_of_Belgian_transsexuals_after_sex_reassig nment_surgery (accessed 24 April 2018).

8. Lawrence S. Mayer, and Paul R. McHugh, The New Atlantis, "Special Report: Sexuality and Gender," https://www.the newatlantis.com/docLib/20160819_TNA50SexualityandG ender.pdf (accessed 22 April 2018).

9. Cakeworld, "Gender, sex and all that > What helps? > References 9: Sex reassignment surgery helps," http://www.cakeworld.info/transsexualism/what-helps/srs (accessed 22 April 2018).This lists 85 studies showing that the surgery is helpful to the patients.

10. Cecilia Dhejne, et al., PLOS ONE, "Long-Term Follow-Up of Transsexual Persons Undergoing Sex Reassignment Surgery: Cohort Study in Sweden," http://journals.plos.org/plosone/article?id=10.1371/journ al.pone.0016885 (accessed 24 April 2018).

11. Annette Kuhn, et al., Fertility and Sterility, "Quality of life 15 years after sex reassignment surgery for transsexualism," https://www.fertstert.org/article/S0015-0282%2808%29 03838-7/fulltext (accessed 3 May 2018).

12. Mohammad Hassan Murad, et al., Mayo Clinic, "Hormonal therapy and sex reassignment: A systematic review and meta-analysis of quality of life and psychosocial outcomes," https://mayoclinic.pure.elsevier.com/en/publications/hor monal-therapy-and-sex-reassignment-a-systematic-review-and-met (accessed 24 April 2018).

13. HRC, "McHugh Exposed: HRC Launches Website Debunking the Junk Science of Paul McHugh," https://www.hrc.org/press/mchugh-exposed-hrc-launches-website-debunking-the-junk-science-of-paul-mchu (accessed 5 May 2018).

14. HRC, "McHugh Exposed: How anti-LGBTQ activists are leveraging junk science to advance their agenda." https://www.hrc.org/mchughexposed (accessed 5 May 2018).

15. Michael Schulson, Undark, "Of Politics, Science, and Gender Identity: The views of the Johns Hopkins psychiatrist Paul R. McHugh on LGBTQ identities seem to turn scientific nuance into a partisan fog."

https://undark.org/article/gender-lgbtq-paul-mchugh-science/ (accessed 5 May 2018).

16. Chris Beyrer, et al., The Baltimore Sun, "Hopkins faculty disavow 'troubling' report on gender and sexuality," http://www.baltimoresun.com/news/opinion/oped/bs-ed-lgbtq-hopkins-20160928-story.html (accessed 23 April 2018).

17. Samantha Allen, Daily Beast, "Anti-LGBT Doc Paul McHugh: I Will Not Be Silenced," https://www.the dailybeast.com/anti-lgbt-doc-paul-mchugh-i-will-not-be-silenced (accessed 23 April 2018).

18. SPLC, "American College of Pediatricians," https://www.splcenter.org/fighting-hate/extremist-files/group/american-college-pediatricians (accessed 22 April 2018).

19. Ana Brown, Pew Research Center, "Republicans, Democrats have starkly different views on transgender issues," http://www.pewresearch.org/fact-tank/2017/11/08/transgender-issues-divide-republicans-and-democrats/ (accessed 3 May 2018).

20. Jonathan V. Last, The Weekly Standard, "Ryan Anderson: Having Genital Preferences Is Now 'Transphobic'," https://www.weeklystandard.com/jonathan-v-last/ryan-anderson-having-genital-preferences-is-now-transphobic (accessed 7 May 2018).

Picture Credits

Page 2. Facepalm. Caïn venant de tuer son frère Abel, by Henri Vidal in Tuileries Garden in Paris, France. This image was originally posted to Flickr by Alex E. Proimos at https://www.flickr.com/photos/34120957@N04/4199675334. It was reviewed on 4 November 2012 by FlickreviewR and was confirmed to be licensed under the terms of the cc-by-2.0. https://commons.wikimedia.org/wiki/File:Paris_Tuileries_G arden_Facepalm_statue.jpg (accessed 9 May 2018).

Page 6. Civil War soldier Albert Cashier. This media file is in the public domain in the United States. https://commons.wikimedia.org/wiki/File:Albert-Cashier.jpg (accessed 9 May 2018).

Page 14. Trans people in restrooms. Popular meme available in many places. https://imgur.com/gallery/WyZoRre (accessed 9 May 2018).

Page 119. Jean Renoir. Paintings by Pierre-Auguste Renoir in the Art Institute of Chicago. This file is licensed under the Creative Commons Attribution 3.0 Unported license, by Sailko. https://commons.wikimedia.org/wiki/File:Pierre-auguste_ renoir,_jean_renoir_che_cuce,_1899-1900.jpg (accessed 9 May 2018).

Page 119. Claude Renoir. Claude Renoir, jouant. Painting by Pierre-Auguste Renoir. This is a faithful photographic reproduction of a two-dimensional, public domain work of art. https://commons.wikimedia.org/wiki/File:Pierre-Auguste_ Renoir_-_Claude_Renoir,_jouant.jpg (accessed 9 May 2018).

Page 120: FDR. A photograph of Franklin Delano Roosevelt at age 2 1/2, illustrating typical gender-neutral clothing at the time. This media file is in the public domain in the United States. https://commons.wikimedia.org/wiki/File:Franklin-Roosevelt-1884.jpg (accessed 9 May 2018).

Page 129. The Gender Unicorn. Design by Landyn Pan and Anna Moore. Trans Student Educational Resources. http://www.transstudent.org/gender (accessed 9 May 2018).

Page 136. Yelled at or beat up. Advocate, "New App Helps Find Safe Bathroom for LGBT Users." https://www.advocate.com/arts-entertainment/internet/2012/08/04/new-app-helps-find-safe-bathroom-lgbt-users (accessed 9 May 2018).

Page 137. Access to Lockers and Showers Under Obama Administration Guidance. Kelly R. Novak, based on logic by Ryan T. Anderson. The Heritage Foundation, "Gender Identity Policies in Schools: What Congress, the Courts, and the Trump Administration Should Do," https://www.heritage.org/education/report/gender-identity-policies-schools-what-congress-the-courts-and-the-trump. Redrawn to match other charts in this chapter. (accessed 9 May 2018).

Pages 137 and 138. Other logic charts. Kelly R. Novak.

Page 140. The new Choices. From a tweet by @Cailin_Becoming on March 13, 2015. Reposted several places, including https://mic.com/articles/114066/statistics-show-exactly-how-many-times-trans-people-have-attacked-you-in-bathrooms#.ILEfcq7RS (accessed 9 May 2018).

Page 141. Photo of Laurence Fishburne from Wikimedia Commons. https://commons.wikimedia.org/wiki/File:National_Memorial_Day_Concert_2017_(34117818524)_(cropped).jpg (accessed 29 April 2018).

Page 152. Mike Pence. This caricature is of Mike Pence was adapted from a photo in the public domain by Barry Bahler from the FEMA Photo Library via Wikimedia. This image was originally posted to Flickr by DonkeyHotey at https://flickr.com/photos/47422005@N04/16913402936. It was reviewed on 16 July 2016 by FlickreviewR and was confirmed to be licensed under the terms of the cc-by-2.0. This file is licensed under the Creative Commons Attribution 2.0 Generic license. https://commons.wikimedia.org/wiki/File: Mike_Pence_-_Caricature.jpg (accessed 9 May 2018).

Page 176. I can't hear you. Portrait eines Mädchens, welches sich die Ohren zuhält beim, by Roger and Renate Rössing, 1954. This file is licensed under the Creative Commons Attribution-Share Alike 3.0 Germany license. https://commons. wikimedia.org/wiki/File:Fotothek_df_roe-neg_0006637_007 _Portrait_eines_M%C3%A4dchens,_welches_sich_die_Ohre n.jpg (accessed 9 May 2018).

Page 187. Dinner Party. The end of dinner, by Jules-Alexandre Grün, 1913. This work is in the public domain in its country of origin and other countries and areas where the copyright term is the author's life plus 70 years or less. https://commons.wikimedia.org/wiki/File:Gr%C3%BCn_-_ _The_End_of_Dinner.jpg (accessed 9 May 2018).

Cover. Male profile. Male and female silhouettes facing away from each other. Source: https://pixabay.com/en/breakup-divorce-separation-908714/. Author: Tumisu. This file is from Pixabay, where the creator has released it explicitly under the license Creative Commons Zero. This file is made available under the Creative Commons CC0 1.0 Universal Public Domain Dedication. https://commons.wikimedia.org/wiki/File:Break up-908714_1280.jpg. (accessed 9 May 2018). Female profile: Pixabay. CC0 Creative Commons. Free for commercial use. No attribution required. https://pixabay.com/en/female-woman-profile-abstract-art-2747374/ (accessed 12 May 2018).

Wikimedia files are in the Public Domain in the USA. ©

227

CPSIA information can be obtained
at www.ICGtesting.com
Printed in the USA
LVHW091453151219
640589LV00001B/30/P

9 781948 785051